Praise for

MW00614741

Internal Tech Conferences

"Simple, clear advice on how to run a successful internal conference, with practical tips and even a toolkit to help. Written by people that have actually done it."

— *Mark Barnes, Foundation Services Technical Officer, Financial Times*

"Running an internal tech conference has made a big contribution to changes in culture and approach at the Financial Times. We aren't the only place who have seen this type of impact. If you want a practical guide to how to do something similar in your organisation, this book is for you!"

— *Sarah Wells, Technical Director for Operations and Reliability, Financial Times*

"We've found internal tech conferences to be transformational for our software development teams and Victoria & Matthew's book provides valuable, practical guidance that will help you plan, run and capitalise on your own brilliant conference."

— *Chris Smith, Head of Product Delivery, Redgate Software*

"Internal Tech Conferences is full of great stories and tips based on real-life experiences and lessons learned which will benefit conference organisers who wish to create a more collaborative and playful workplace through shared learning."

— *Portia Tung, Executive Agile Coach, Play Researcher and founder of The School of Play (www.theschoolofplay.org), dedicated to promoting happier adulthood through lifelong play*

"At IDBS we build some complicated software for the life science sector using a wide range of technologies, so it's vital that all our engineers are always up to speed on the different approaches and techniques. In 2019 we ran the first of our Eng.age events, an internal conference for all engineers working on our software products. Over 20 people presented topics ranging from AI/ML, Serverless, UX in Scrum, blockchain, performance testing to GraphQL. We used the excellent ideas and patterns in the book Internal Tech Conferences to help us plan, execute, and follow-up on the conference. The book was hugely useful for making our internal tech conference a success - in particular, the checklists at the back of the book helped us to avoid a whole set of non-obvious problems, making the day run smoothly."

— *Wesley Childs, Senior Director of Engineering, IDBS*

Internal Tech Conferences
Accelerate Multi-team Learning

Victoria Morgan-Smith and Matthew Skelton

Conflux Books

Leeds, UK

Internal Tech Conferences
Accelerate Multi-team Learning

Victoria Morgan-Smith and
Matthew Skelton

Published by Conflux Books, a trading name of Conflux Digital Ltd, Leeds, UK.

Commissioning Editor: Matthew Skelton
Cover Design: Matthew Oglesby

For information about bulk discounts or booking the authors for an event, please email info@confluxbooks.com

ISBN   978-1-912058-83-9
eBook ISBN 978-1-912058-97-6
Kindle ISBN 978-1-912058-82-2
PDF ISBN   978-1-912058-74-7

Conflux Books: confluxbooks.com

Contents

Conflux Books

Books for technologists by technologists

Our books help to accelerate and deepen your learning in the field of software systems. We focus on subjects that don't go out of date: fundamental software principles & practices, team interactions, and technology-independent skills.

Current and planned titles in the *Conflux Books* series include:

1. *Build Quality In* edited by Steve Smith and Matthew Skelton (B01)
2. *Better Whiteboard Sketches* by Matthew Skelton (B02)
3. *Internal Tech Conferences* by Victoria Morgan-Smith and Matthew Skelton (B03)
4. *Technical Writing for Blogs and Articles* by Matthew Skelton (B04)

 Find out more about the *Conflux Books* series by visiting: confluxbooks.com

Acknowledgements

We would like to thank the following people for their help and involvement in the writing of this book: Calum Loudon at Metaswitch; Rik Still and Mark Barnes at FT; Andrew Betts at EdgeConf for his experience and advice on running panel discussions; Thurston Tye & Michael Huniewicz at FT (photography); James Hamill and Ben Morgan-Smith for editorial assistance; Ben Maraney, Case Taintor, Kim Oberg, and Matthias Feist at Klarna; Rich Haigh (formerly of Paddy Power Betfair); the PIPELINE Conference team (Amy Phillips, Anthony Green, Beccy Stafford, Chris O'Dell, Inka Howorth, and Steve Smith).

We'd like to extend special thanks to Manuel Pais for editing the original InfoQ article *Internal Tech Conferences* in 2016 and including it in the 2017 InfoQ eMag *Scaling DevOps*.

We also give a big "thank you" to our reviewers: Ben Maraney, David Legge, Emily Webber, Mark Dalgarno, Portia Tung.

Some icons are made by made by Freepik from www.flaticon.com - icons used in accordance with the Flaticon license terms

Introduction

Internal tech conferences can make a significant impact on an organisation's level of sharing, learning, and communication by accelerating multi-team learning across technology departments. An increasing number of enlightened organisations are using this powerful approach to spread and embed new ideas and practices.

In this book we share practical advice on how to prepare, run, and follow-up on an internal tech conference, together with some case studies from several organisations showing the approaches in common and the adaptations for each situation.

How to use this book

This book is for people involved in technology leadership in some form: people in "official" positions of leadership (CIO, CTO, Head of Engineering, IT Operations Manager, etc.) and those in more informal technology leadership positions, such as team leaders, senior engineers, and people who simply like to lead by example. Having been in such positions ourselves, we (Victoria and Matthew) want to help other technology leaders to devise and run successful internal tech conferences to act as a key strategic differentiator for organisations building software systems.

- **Chapter 1** gives an overview of internal tech conferences and why you might want to run such an event. Read this chapter **if you have never run or experienced an internal tech conference before** to help you understand the purpose and the things involved.
- **Chapter 2** explains how to prepare for an internal tech conference. Read this to understand **what is involved, how long the preparation takes, and what kind of team you will need** to make the conference happen.
- **Chapter 3** covers the conference day itself. Read this chapter to understand **all the operational aspects of the conference** and to see what kind of help you may need on the day.
- **Chapter 4** deals with the weeks and months following the conference. Read this chapter to see how to get the most out of the day by **following up on talks and panel sessions** and how to ensure that the conferences are **an opportunity for learning and growth**.
- **Chapter 5** contains detailed **case studies** from a selected group of organisations. This chapter is different from the others in that the material is presented in a more linear, retrospective fashion (more like a story). Read this chapter to get a feel for **how real organisations have run internal tech conferences** and what they learned.
- The **Toolkit** at the back of the book contains tools and templates for planning and running an internal tech conference; these can be used and adapted as needed.

Chapters 1 to 4 deliberately read as "how-to" guides with quite specific recommendations. Chapter 5 has a more narrative flavour, befitting the case study stories. The Toolkit provides some templates and quick-start guides for getting results quickly.

Why we wrote this book

We met (appropriately) at a conference in 2015 where Victoria gave a talk about some early changes at Financial TImes to create a learning organisation. We realised that we both had some similar experience of organising and running internal tech conferences and decided to write an article, published by InfoQ in 2016 [1]. As far as we could tell, this was the first online article to cover all aspects of internal tech conferences in detail, comparing approaches from different organisations, and it was included in the InfoQ eMag *Scaling DevOps* in May 2017 [2].

Since the article was published, we have been happy to see several new online articles covering internal tech conferences, and we know from speaking to people in the industry (at least in the UK) that the approach is becoming more widespread. We therefore decided to write this book to provide a template and set of guidelines for not just running the conference itself but how to go about preparing for one and how to get the most strategic and tactical value out of a series of conferences.

About the authors

 Victoria Morgan-Smith is Director of Delivery, Internal Products at the Financial Times, where she has been helping teams succeed since 2009. Before this she was a developer for 9 years, a background which fuels her interest in finding fun ways to coach, energise and motivate teams into self-organising units. She is passionate about collaboration beyond the team, adopting agile principles to get under the skin of what will deliver measurable business value around the organisation.

Twitter: @VictoriaJMS | LinkedIn: victoriamorgansmith

 Matthew Skelton is Head of Consulting at Conflux (confluxdigital.net), where he specialises in Continuous Delivery, operability and organisation dynamics for software in manufacturing, ecommerce, and online services. Recognised by TechBeacon in 2018 as one of the top 100 people to follow in DevOps, Matthew curates the well-known DevOps team topologies patterns at devopstopologies.com and is co-author of the books *Continuous Delivery with Windows and .NET* (O'Reilly, 2016), *Team Guide to Software Operability* (Skelton Thatcher Publications, 2016), and *Team Topologies* (IT Revolution Press, 2019).

Twitter: @matthewpskelton | confluxdigital.net

1. Benefits - why run an internal tech conference

This chapter will help you to answer these questions:

- What measurable benefits would we gain from running an internal tech conference?
- How would an event like this tie in to my broader organisational goals?
- What can this event do for the personal development of my employees?
- What different approaches should I consider?
- Is this something I want to invest in?

1.1 What is an internal tech conference?

An internal tech conference is effectively a technology conference run by and for the staff of a single organisation. Done well - as suggested by this book - an internal tech conference helps to bring together disparate teams and individuals in a shared celebration and examination of the current practices and approaches within the organisation, accelerating learning at a time of rapid technological change.

The conference could be a half-day event, a single day, or multiple days; it might be every few months or just once per year. Speakers and conference organisers alike are drawn from within the organisation, making the day a real "team effort". The focus is on learning and improving together as an organisation in a setting where sometimes-sensitive details can be shared openly with colleagues. With many public tech conference tickets costing upwards of €800-1000 per person, many organisations find that an internal tech conference is a highly cost-effective way of training and developing staff whilst simultaneously improving cohesion and camaraderie.

1.2 The business case

Modern software development has co-evolved with cloud and IoT technologies to become a vital part of how successful organisations do business. Gone are the days of "death march" software projects; instead we have long-term product-based or service-based ownership of business services and user experiences, all enabled by rapid infrastructure provisioning, ubiquitous automation, and high-fidelity instrumentation and telemetry.

Software delivery approaches such as Lean Agile and DevOps have demonstrated convincingly the value and power of focused collaboration on key aspects of technology and user need. Research from industry experts such as DORA and Google has shown that organisations that invest in technical and social practices for their teams consistently perform better than other organisations [46] [47]. Internal tech conferences are an excellent way to invest in team social practices.

In their 2018 book *Accelerate*, authors Nicole Forsgren and colleagues identify some key drivers of organisational performance, based on research involving thousands of organisations worldwide. Their research show that staff loyalty and how well members of staff identify with the mission of the organisation are important components of high organisational performance [48].

We believe that internal tech conferences are one of the best ways to increase staff loyalty and identification with organisational goals for several reasons that we'll explore in this book:

1. People see their work celebrated and validated within the organisation
2. People see their colleagues and coworkers on-stage, presenting their work in a compelling way, and can be inspired to do the same
3. People have a chance to reflect on recent achievements and consolidate their understanding of recent changes

4. People can see that the organisation is investing in learning and development in a very visible way

5. Where organisations run internal tech conferences on a regular basis, people can see that the organisation as a whole takes learning and improvement seriously. Learning and mastery are key to staff motivation [54] so learning helps with loyalty too.

By bringing people together in the same physical or temporal space for an extended period of joint learning, organisations help ideas and approaches to spread and align across many different teams [45]. Increasing inter-team cohesion like this helps to produce a culture of excellence based on mutual learning which in turn increases organisational performance.

1.3 Measurable benefits

An internal tech conference can be a powerful way of communicating and celebrating technology teams that build and operate the software systems that are increasingly essential to many organisations.

An event like this has many immediate, measurable benefits, as well as some hidden, long term ones. One major goal is to shape and promote a culture where people are encouraged to challenge the status quo and to get excited about new possibilities by having the space to experiment without the fear of failure. Psychologically, people are braver surrounded by people they know and trust; an internal tech conference can help people get to know each other in an open context, allowing them to share opinions and ideas.

In our research for this book, we have examined the motivations of many organisations for running this sort of event. For example, employees at Metaswitch say that their conference *"reminds them they work with a great bunch of people"* [3] says Calum Loudon (head of architecture and conference organiser). Investing in a full day for employees to share the things that excite them enables them to appreciate each other afresh and boosts their engagement with the organisation (the full case study from Metaswitch is in Chapter 5).

Other organisations had similar experiences. In fact, three clear themes emerge as reasons for running an internal tech conference: Empowerment, Learning and Connection.

1.4 Empowerment, Learning, Connection

1.4.1 Empowerment

Successful organisations are increasingly finding that a vital part of organisational agility is the empowerment of teams. Giving teams localised autonomy over their work enables a tighter feedback loop between action and results, helping the organisation to self-steer towards better outcomes for customers and users.

If you are looking to introduce a more egalitarian mindset within your organisation - where employees are given more autonomy over how they work, have more opportunity to be creative, are expected to take more accountability for making smart and responsible decisions, then you need to engage them in the bigger picture. Empowerment needs to be taken, not given - and this is a great opportunity to create an atmosphere that will enable that to begin.

It is clear that the traditional model of having senior managers provide all of the answers, expertise and direction is severely limiting. This event can act as an implicit invitation to collaborate with leaders to take collective ownership of your department's health.

Most of the organisations in this book talk about their internal conferences being organised from the bottom up, by ordinary staff. Whilst in some cases there is a clear agenda set by leadership based on a theme they would like to address, many others facilitate an empowered curation of content. In both scenarios - whether leadership are asking the questions, or inviting the room to ask them - they are inviting the department to help *answer* them.

Internal conferences help to open the floor to all people, elevating voices not often heard. People do not necessarily need to be talking about weighty topics, simply the fact of being given the opportunity to design their own day is empowerment in action. Of course, if people do choose to join some debates about some of the options and choices made in terms of technology, ways of working, or department goals and structure, then that's going to have a huge impact on their levels of engagement.

1.4.2 Learning

Building and operating modern software systems is a challenging task: the pace of delivery is rapid and we need to draw on a wide range of skills and experience in a coordinated, joined-up way. As our world changes, and new ways of working and leading emerge, so should new ways of learning. Spending money on sending a handful of people out to public conferences no longer seems to make the impact we need it to, at least alone; public conferences are often too expensive for all staff to attend and they are not tailored to the needs of the organisation or individuals.

Talks, panel discussions and even classroom sessions are all great ways to promote learning at an internal tech conference. Image credit: Matthew Skelton

There are smart people working hard in technology departments the world over - experimenting, discovering new ways of solving problems every day - and yet most organisations tend to look outside for learning. That is of course vital, but what the companies that feature in our case studies have also realised is that if they look at their own employees then they can learn a huge amount without going anywhere at all.

> *Hearing about the approaches other teams have used to solve problems can help you think differently about the challenges you are facing. Learning about how others ensure quality, for instance with different approaches to security, testing, monitoring or deployment, can inspire you to step up your own game. As an extra bonus, at an internal conference, these solutions are more likely to make sense in the context (infrastructure, regulation, culture) in which your organisation operates.*
> - Ben Maraney, formerly of Klarna [50] (Read more about Klarna in Chapter 5.)

Empowerment is closely linked to the shifts in corporate culture that enable *emergent leadership*. It is held that by encouraging self-organisation and self-management, companies will end up with a better-led organisation.

The **Learning 3.0** approach is a response to this. Just as there are better ways to lead an organisation - encouraging everyone to be proactive in their quest to make their company a better place to be - there is also a better way for employees to learn than to passively receive information. In his book *How Creative Workers Learn* Alexandre Magno talks about emergent learning - people learn through experience and interaction, not through consuming reams of pre-prepared material. "Learning emerges from the connection of stories, ideas and practice", he says [5].

Whilst a conference that has the agenda driven externally can teach attendees something "theoretically", an internal conference brings the exciting opportunity to explore ideas and challenges *within the context of the organisation*, with insights coming from the collective and not solely from a few appointed experts.

The Financial Times recognises the value of sending people out to public conferences, but their Engine Room conference *"ensures that we also learn from the brilliant people inside our company."* Cait O'Riordan (CPIO) explains that *"Ideally that would happen anyway in the course of our daily lives - but putting some time in the calendar makes sure that sharing actually happens and happens at scale"* [5].

Furthermore, from the perspective of the speakers, giving a talk means doing a lot of learning themselves. In order to get up and speak authoritatively on a subject, speakers need to do some research into what else is being said in the industry on their chosen topic to validate or update their viewpoints. So this is their opportunity to further enlighten themselves on something. *"Be the protagonist of your own learning"* says Learning 3.0; an internal tech conference should be an enriching experience for speakers to grasp with both hands.

1.4.3 Connection

In the 2019 book *Team Topologies*, Matthew Skelton and Manuel Pais identify the need for regular learning and cross-team knowledge sharing using a range of techniques, especially internal tech conferences [45]. One of the challenges of the increasingly common culture of autonomy is that people often don't take the time to connect with colleagues beyond their immediate team. Agility has seen a move towards self-sufficiency, giving teams the ability to realise the value of their work without depending on anyone else who might slow them down. Although this self-sufficiency is generally positive, it does create its own problems. In particular, the desire by engineers to solve their own problems means that the same problems are often being solved repeatedly in the same department: autonomy without alignment.

There are benefits to connecting with other teams beyond the opportunity to learn and swap stories. It is hugely valuable for people to have the chance to break out from the normal team silos and to encounter other people in a setting that is not defined by project scope or operational problems. The parts of the conference day where the interaction is at its highest - whether it's in an open space discussion, lunchtime chit chat or evening drinks - are in many ways the most important parts of the day.

The informal interaction during the internal tech conference day is where people build up a healthy balance of "*social capital*" [26]. Each time social capital is boosted it is like an influenza jab, inoculating them against later conflict when a more difficult time appears. If people need help from each other, their interaction will be swifter and smoother after spending time chatting at the conference. If they need to present a challenge to one another, they will do so with more humanity. It is said that for technology departments and organisations today the only constant is change, which means that misunderstandings and and conflicts are never far away. Social capital provides a buffer to help people pull together across the department when these changes arise, so anything that builds up those reserves is worthwhile.

Donald Clark's excellent article *Conferences – jumped up*

classrooms? [30] presents a challenge to prevent an internal conference from turning into a scenario where *"people turn up to be spoon-fed by sages on the stage talking at them [...] a lazy approach to learning"*. He urges readers to evoke some emotional response and to not fall into the trap of being a "forgetting experience". For internal tech conferences, avoid anything that feels like pure instruction, and instead seek to stimulate some lively debates that will actively engage employees and trigger some shifts in mindset. The behavioural change that comes with new ways of thinking and seeing others is the lasting effect you can most hope for.

1.5 Define what speakers gain

Speaking in front of a large group of colleagues can be daunting for people, so be clear about the benefits for speakers. Management will also want to understand the advantages of investing time in training and preparing the speakers.

1.5.1 Celebrate unsung heroes

An internal tech conference is a great opportunity to identify and celebrate 'unsung' people, teams, and achievements; it's a way to showcase team projects that might be forgotten or that do less exciting but crucial work. You may decide to deliberately look for people who have done particularly interesting, foundational, or transformative work - such as database upgrades that allowed them to shift platforms or deployment automation that reduced outages - or perhaps someone who can describe in (painful) detail what it's like to be on the 1st-line support team.

1.5.2 Personal growth

Speaking at an internal event will help people to challenge themselves. The opinions they've been expressing on a daily basis to their neighbouring coworkers will need to be fact-checked if they want to express them on stage, then do a bit more research to be sure they know what they're talking about. A team can easily become a small echo chamber, so it's healthy for people to raise their head occasionally. Then they can say, "Hey, it's not just me - other people are saying this stuff too!". Many conference speakers will tell you that the biggest thing they get out of talking at an event is the extra learning they do in order to test and flesh out their message.

1.5.3 Confidence

To many people, public speaking is the most terrifying experience in the world; consequently many great ideas and opinions remain unheard. If an internal tech conference can help people tackle that fear of speaking, that's a huge gift. As we see in Chapter 5, many people go on to talk at external conferences as a direct result of gaining confidence to do so at internal events.

1.6 Define what attendees gain

Attendees at a well-run internal tech conference should receive a huge boost to their awareness and enthusiasm for their work, but how do they know this beforehand? Take the time to spell out exactly how attendees will benefit.

1.6.1 Engagement with the organisation

One of the big benefits for attendees is the buzz of sharing insight and successes; this makes an organisation feel like a great place to work. The organisations in our case studies have all reported a general boost in morale after these events, as the chance to take time out and think about things in a different way and to hear inspirational stories from each other gave employees a renewed connection with the company.

1.6.2 Feeling valued

Metaswitch ran in-depth workshops that last 2-3 hours giving people a chance to get stuck into the new technologies like the Internet of Things - in parallel to talks on both tech and non-tech subjects, thus delivering something for everyone. Across disciplines, attendees felt a strong sense that they were considered worth investing in.

1.6.3 Learning and validation

Another benefit of internal tech conferences can be the validation that comes from hearing colleagues talk about practices used elsewhere in the industry too. Encourage some speakers to talk about practices in other organisations by referring to books they have read or talks they have seen. By bringing a piece of the outside world into a company, everyone gains a better understanding of how their shared work makes up a bigger picture. Often this involves reinforcing that they're doing the right things already - a big motivation.

1.7 What types of events work?

There are several options for the type of event you run. The format you choose will depend on what outcomes you seek from your event, as you can get quite different results with each format. The following examples provide a flavour of the different kinds of events that have been proven to work well.

1.7.1 Financial Times: 1-day annual event with internal speakers only

The Financial Times (FT) is a global news organisation with roots in London, UK. The FT team decided to run a full day event with a mixture of content and debate from a diverse set of people across the department, joined solely by an internal audience. The conference consisted of Lightning Talks, Panel Debates, Open Spaces and a game, rounded off with beer, chatter, and more beer. The conversation-based sessions proved hugely successful at capturing the mood and stimulating changes in the department [7].

A lively panel discussion at FT during their first internal tech conference. Image credit: Thurston Tye

A panel at the FT's Engine Room Live event get ready for a question on its way from the audience - complete with soft blue throwable microphone [8]!

1.7.2 Metaswitch: 2-day annual event with internal speakers and "friends"

Metaswitch, a software for telecommunications company, ran an energetic multi-stream 2-day event, incorporating a mixture of full-length talks and workshops, with team-led social events in the evenings. The audience is almost entirely internal, but with a few "friends of Metaswitch" as guest speakers. It's described as a highlight in the company calendar, and has directly influenced employee engagement within the engineering department.

1.7.3 Klarna: 1-day internal off-site event for all in engineering

Klarna is a major European bank based in Sweden. Since 2014 Klarna has run an annual 1-day internal tech conference in Stockholm, bringing together an increasingly large engineering community to share ideas and discover new approaches.

Klarna found that by mentoring and training their own staff in speaking and writing talks, the quality of talk submissions has grown each year. All speakers are now drawn from within Klarna and this helps to make the event highly relevant for all attendees [10]. The main conference (attended by everyone) is a 1-day event, but Klarna also use the day before the conference for additional workshops and roundtable sessions for smaller groups; this is the only time in the year when they have all the engineers in one place.

Read more about the Klarna, Metaswitch and FT examples in the Case Studies in Chapter 5.

1.7.4 Paddy Power Betfair: off-site, with some external speakers

Other organisations have found different formats that work well for them. For instance, the online betting and gaming company Paddy Power Betfair hold an annual DevOps Community conference for everyone in Product and Technology [11]. Rich Haigh, former Head of Delivery Enablement at Paddy Power Betfair, explains:

> "*On the morning we invite vendors to come and talk about how we have used their products – what's coming up in their roadmaps, etc. In the afternoon we open the floor to talk about projects they have been working on, interesting tech, R&D they are doing, etc. We then have a social event in the evening. ... We hire an external venue ... and we video everything so we can share the knowledge further after the event.*"

1.7.5 ING: internal and external speakers, with a specific theme

At the Dutch bank ING, an internal change from older, silo-based ways of working to a more fluid, DevOps-inspired approach was accelerated by running an internal conference based directly on the DevOpsDays conference format, combining external invited speakers, internal talks, and short 'lightning' talks of 5 mins each. This event helped to "stir up the discussion" around new ways of working and inspired people to attend and help organise a public conference (DevOpsDays Amsterdam) [12].

Furthermore, after the ING people blogged about their conference and shared the slides, a team at US retailer Target were inspired to run their own conference [28]. The recently-published *DevOps Handbook* by Gene Kim et al has more on the approach at Target [40].

1.7.6 UK-based ticket retailer: 6 monthly half-day event, all staff invited

An online ticket retailer in the UK opted to invite teams outside of technology to learn what the tech teams actually did, as that was a mystery to many people; the sessions were known as 'Engineering Day'. All staff in the London office were invited. The first installment was a full day session with many different speakers from the engineering teams (and some from other departments too). Subsequently, the team ran focused half-day Engineering Day events every six months which allowed more people to attend as they found it easier to spare a half day rather than a full day. Teams in

India were included via video conference and eventually the show went 'on the road' to the teams in Edinburgh [9].

Consider an "unconference" if your organisational culture is right. An unconference is a learning event that prioritises peer-to-peer learning, usually with a schedule developed on the day itself by the participants. This format works well in situations where those involved are confident about presenting and sharing ideas [55].

1.7.7 Permission to pause

There is no 'right way' to run an internal tech conference - it depends on what your team, department or organisation needs. An important thing to consider early on is the audience: who should we invite? Who would benefit most from the conference? The answers to those questions should help to frame your conference planning: as the attendee list grows the focal point of discussions stretches to fit the audience, whereas a more compact group of attendees allows the focus and aims of the conference to remain tighter.

However you choose to run your internal conference, it's important to give people enough time and space to immerse themselves in the event: help people clear their calendars so they can 'shake the every-day out of their hair'. This is a chance for people to give themselves permission to pause - they need to be ready to get as much out of the day as possible.

1.8 Learn from external events

Much can be learned from looking to successful external (public) conferences for inspiration. In a blog post *How to run a good tech conference* [44], Matthew Skelton identifies nine key things to address:

1. Find a fabulous organising team
2. Choose a venue wisely
3. Make the conference practitioner-led
4. Make the conference inclusive
5. Find good sponsors and suppliers
6. Plan the money side carefully
7. Use a decent ticketing platform
8. Treat all people involved with respect
9. Find great keynote speakers

Of these nine points, only point 5 (sponsors and suppliers) and point 7 (ticketing) do not really apply to an internal conference. A strong and passionate organising team is essential (see Chapter 2). You may be restricted to company offices for the venue, but if you have the option of hiring an out-of-office venue, look for a venue that does not "split up" the conference, so that every one of the attendees can feel part of the same shared experience.

Build the organising team with representatives from across your engineering organisation. This is particularly important for the people who solicit and review talk proposals. If attendees know that the organisers and speakers are practitioners like them, they interact as equals and feel able to share more; make sure to encourage practitioners to get involved, particularly those who are from underrepresented groups or those who have not spoken before. An inclusive, diverse conference will generate better engagement and discussions than a conference with the same faces that always speak.

As we have seen, many of the challenges and activities between external and internal conferences are similar, but there are some differences that are worth bearing in mind, which we explore in the following sections.

1.8.1 Tickets

External conferences generally have two sources of income to cover the costs of their event: ticket revenue and sponsorship. For an internal conference it's unlikely that you would want to charge your employees money to attend your conference. You might use a ticketing platform for convenience, but keep the tickets free.

1.8.2 Sponsorship

Whilst sponsorship for your internal conference might be possible, it is something to approach with caution. Your conference is probably focused on things that are core to your organisation and will most likely only include external people as guests. As such it is unlikely to be appropriate to introduce someone else's brand/context to your event or hugely beneficial to any potential sponsor; you should expect costs to be covered entirely by departmental/divisional budget. Use the example budget in the Toolkit to help you establish what the budget should be and adjust your plans accordingly.

1.8.3 Marketing

An internal conference will need some marketing and promotion to attract staff but probably not to the same degree as an external conference. Consider how to create a "buzz" around the event without making things too polished or formal. Whether people are expected to attend or the conference is optional, how can you make it exciting or interesting?

1.8.4 Publicity

The organisation probably expects some kind of positive publicity from the internal conference, but you will need to be careful with some of the photographs, videos, and details - it's likely that some of the material in the talks will be confidential or for internal-use only. At a public/external conference, it's normally safe to assume that all the material has been checked for sensitivity, but this is not the case with internal conferences. Check with relevant people before publishing details of talks. Of course, the fact that you are running an internal tech conference should be something to publicise; make people want to join the organisation so they get to find out more details about the talks!

1.9 Chapter Review

Every organisation is different, and what you decide to do will be dependent upon your context. Use the ideas here to help you decide what you want to do.

Some benefits are "tangible" and immediately measurable:

- Working groups forming to tackle a cross-team problem
- Projects transformed through "lightbulb" moments
- Social capital injection avoiding wasted time and energy in future conflicts

Ask yourself: What tangible benefits would you hope to see from your event? And how will you measure them?

Other benefits are harder to measure, but arguably far more significant:

- Empowerment - and the resulting responsibility
- Learning - peer-education, shared lessons
- Connection - improved relationships and collaboration

Ask yourself: What goals do you have in your department that would benefit from improved inter-team relationships?

Provide lots of opportunity for personal development:

- Participants - confidence, public speaking skills, grasp of their chosen topic
- Attendees - engagement, new knowledge, relationships, validation
- All - sense of being valued

Ask yourself: In what ways would you like your employees to grow and develop? How can you use this event to help them do this?

Choose the approach that will give you the outcome you want:

- "By the people, for the people" - a bottom-up approach
- A specific theme for the day
- Showcase your group to the rest of your organisation

Ask yourself: What do you want to achieve from this event? What opportunities or constraints might you have that help determine your approach?

Decide whether this is something for you:

Consider how you could experiment and learn whether this is really for you. Set a limited budget, run it once, and review whether to scale up or down the following year.

Ask yourself: How much are you willing to invest in this?

2. Preparing for the conference

This chapter will help you to answer these questions:

- How do we get started?
- What format and structure should we have?
- How do we choose our speakers?
- What planning activities are involved?
- How do we inspire employees to attend?

2.1 Get buy-in from senior management

Buy-in from senior management is an essential first step for a successful internal tech conference, even if your conference is organised bottom-up as a grassroots effort. As Ben Maraney says in his series of articles about running an internal conference, you need two things from senior management: *"The first is simple approval: a budget and permission to work on the project. The second is true buy-in and support. This means making it clear … that everyone should be able to attend … and that speakers and organisers should be encouraged to invest time and energy in preparing for the event"* [10].

Be very clear about what you want to achieve with the event. You will need to articulate clearly to senior management:

- The benefits your department can expect to see
- Examples of other events at other organisations where it has been considered successful (hopefully some of the content from this book can help you)
- An idea of what a potential agenda might be
- An idea of the budget you will need

> The Toolkit later in this book has some useful templates to help you prepare for the meeting with senior management.

2.1.1 Sell the benefits

The main benefits of an internal tech conference are ultimately enhanced organisational capabilities rooted in social relations: improved interaction, trust and understanding between people and teams. Selling the value of the event may simply be a matter of selling the importance of these aspects to your work environment.

The benefits of internal tech conferences seen in the case studies (Chapter 5) include:

- **Smoother collaboration**: staff organising rotations in each others' teams
- **Improved learning**: a significant increase in lunchtime or evening tech talks; engineers self-organising regular open discussion sessions.
- **Increased engagement**: working groups set up by engineers to delve into particular challenges
- **Inter-team communication**: improved communication between the technology department and the rest of the organisation, opening up a dialogue that may not have been possible before the event
- **Inspiration**: someone from another department, inspired by what they'd heard, taking back to their team a long list of ideas for how they could collaborate better with the tech team [29]
- **Staff retention and recruitment**: speakers taking to the stage at external events, which in turn has brought good candidates applying for jobs

2.2 Form a strong organising team for the event

Having people in the team that are passionate about the conference is crucial. There is a lot of fairly boring work that "just needs to happen" and so you need people with intrinsic motivation to pull together the conference. Have practical people who are ready to "get stuck in" and take responsibility for tasks such as creating and populating a promotional website, making posters, sweet-talking speakers, organising the catering, etc. And you need a "chief worrier" who is just good at finding the blind-spots.

Whilst your team should be small - too large a group can invoke the worst type of collective ownership (which can mean no-one owns things at all) - you need to know who else you can call on for specific things that you need help with, so have someone on your team who knows the organisation well. A core organising group of 3-5 people seems to work well for many organisations. Make your conference organising committee represent the diversity of your engineering workforce to ensure a well-balanced event [13].

Don't forget that beyond your core team you will need help and input from lots of other useful people. As with many things, people will get out of this conference what they put in - so the more you can involve everyone in the up front contribution of ideas, organisation and actually taking part in the day, the more they will feel it is "for them" and the more they will take away from the event.

2.3 Choose the date and venue

Choose a date at least 3 months ahead (and preferably 6 months or more). Once you have a date, you have a deadline to work back from in terms of planning your activities. The planning and preparation will take around 3-6 months of elapsed time.

The main reason for giving yourselves at least 3 months is that you need to give your speakers enough time to prepare - emotionally as well as practically - so engaging them should be something you aim to do as soon as you can.

The other time-critical element tends to be booking the venue. Even if you are using internal facilities, there is a good chance that those big rooms get booked up well in advance, so securing the rooms is key to reducing last-minute panics.

Consider the effect on attendees of the conference venue: will attendees need to book travel and accommodation? How will this work logistically? Travel and accommodation costs can form a significant part of the conference budget, so get clarity on this aspect early on.

2.4 Choose the right format

There are many different formats for an internal tech conference that work well (see **What types of events work?** in Chapter 1). It is important to consider what would work well in your situation.

2.4.1 Ask yourself what type of activities would be best for you. What do you want to achieve?

- Do you want to generate debate, or do you want to educate/inform?
- Do you want to stimulate discussion amongst your engineers, or do you want to show them off to the rest of the organisation?
- Do you want external speakers, or should they all be internal?
- Does the venue available to you impose any constraints (or suggest any options)?
- Do you have remote offices to include, and does this affect the options available to you?

Whatever your answers to these questions, you should incorporate different types of activities, as different people have preferences for different types of sessions. Some may prefer to listen to a talk, others may enjoy firing questions at a panel, or learning a new technique with a hands-on workshop. Try to include a variety of sessions to keep things lively.

2.4.1.1 Different activities you could include:

Lightning Talks

A 5-10 minute talk is so short that it **encourages the speaker to get to the point quickly**! And they work well for periods of the day when energy is low - the kickoff, post-lunch, or wrap-up.

For an extra challenge, try the PechaKucha 20x20 format [15], where slides go on auto-play!

Open Spaces

Break-out discussions on specific topics (either chosen in advance or generated on the day by inviting people to volunteer to host a session) can be great to **stimulate broader discussion**. They work well during breaks or lunch, when people are milling around and ready to talk whilst they eat.

Longer talks

A 45-60 minute talk provides the opportunity to **really get into a topic**, and Metaswitch find this their most popular format altogether. A good talk can mean people walk away inspired having learnt something tangible - especially if you have a good Q&A mechanism set up.

Workshops

If you have the space, enabling people to learn something hands-on can work very well for **engaging people in something new and exciting**. If you don't have space in the schedule or venue to do this, then you could choose to do a Lightning Talk to promote a workshop on a later date. The day before or after the main conference is a good time to run workshops, because everyone is in the same location already so no additional travel is needed.

Training taster sessions

Introductory courses in coding or using new tools can appeal to a wide range of people, particularly those whose job does not normally cover these areas.

Panel discussions

A structured panel discussion with (some) pre-curated questions, using tools that surface real-time responses and further questions from the audience, can be energetic and hugely powerful. This can work well for opening up questions that have been rumbling around under the surface and giving them a good airing. The Financial Times found this a tremendously effective format (see Chapter 5).

If you take this route, remember that **the purpose of panels is to provoke**, which makes them ideal if your conference goals include trying to surface more than the opinions of a handful of speakers.

> For more details on why panels are a fantastic mechanism and how to make them work well, we recommend reading Andrew Betts' excellent article on *Better Developer Conferences* [31], where he describes how he shaped this for EdgeConf - the inspiration for the FT's format. Additionally, there are guides in the Toolkit section at the back of this book on how to moderate panels successfully.

Games

Finishing the day with a game, some food and some drink can set everyone up for the all important after-event drinks, **where the real networking takes place**. The FT have played word games like "Just A Minute" (based on a BBC Radio 2 panel game), Metaswitch have run team quizzes, Lindyhop dancing and a home-made team challenge game based on the popular TV show "Crystal Maze" (from the UK). The possibilities are endless here!

Open Space discussion at the FT's Engine Room event

EXTERNAL SPEAKERS - YES OR NO?

External speakers can lend a sense of excitement to the conference but can also distract from goals of bringing together the workforce. Consider also whether you have an objective of giving people a voice and letting them know they are heard - would bringing in external speakers distract from this? Metaswitch have brought in an occasional external speaker - ex-employees and close connections. Their multi-streamed event meant that one or two external speakers added an extra dimension to the event without damaging the "safe space" ethos.

Consider the type of space you want to create. How important is it to you that you maintain safety and security - not only in terms of feeling safe to fail, but also in terms of confidentiality?

Taken to the extreme, bringing external speakers in can be a bit like bringing an industry conference to all of your employees without the expense of flying your whole organisation out to it. There's a big incentive to doing this, but it's important to be aware of the trade-offs. It really comes down to what you want to achieve with the day. You should expect to pay any external speakers, so include this in your budget.

2.5 Identify your speakers

It's important to be inclusive - you're trying to inspire people by amplifying good ideas and discussions, and so your speakers need to be representative. You want that to include some of the quieter people who have fantastic ideas that don't usually get heard - but be prepared for the likelihood that less experienced speakers will be slow to volunteer, whilst those who do this often will continue to put themselves forward. You will need to work on providing a non-intimidating and supportive atmosphere in order to attract new voices.

A good approach is:

- Start with people who are keen and have something interesting to say
- Consider the mix of speakers: are different groups well-represented?
- Go and spend some time persuading "missing" people to talk at the conference. Communicate that you're offering training and mentoring to help them prepare a talk.

It might take several iterations of the event to achieve a good representative mix of speakers, so don't obsess about getting this right first time. Less represented people and less confident people may need to see evidence that the event is well-run before volunteering.

Correlation between diversity and business success

Having a diverse range of speakers is not merely "the right thing to do", it's good for your business too. Research shows a direct and positive correlation between diversity and success in an organisation. [14] More diversity leads to a broader perspective, more creativity and ultimately more profit. Showcasing a diverse range of people is likely to help the organisation to thrive.

The more welcoming your working environment, the fewer barriers there are to people wishing to join you. So, *accepting that a diverse workplace is the right thing for your organisation*, then we recommend that your conference line-up reflects this. Ensure that the speaker group is inclusive of all your department; in this way everyone should feel represented and inclined to contribute both to the event itself and also to any follow-up activities.

2.5.1 Launch a Call for Papers

You need to put out a call for talks (sometimes called a "Call for Papers", or CfP). A simple online form asking a few questions is probably all you need to find keen people. You may decide to provide some criteria as to what you think makes a "good" talk. For Metaswitch it simply comes down to "something they think other people would be interested in", but you may have other criteria - particularly if you have a theme in mind for the day. An advantage with having clear and published criteria is that it makes it easy to explain to someone why their talk wasn't selected.

You'll need to collect some basic information, including:

- Presenter Name
- Email Address (to contact them again)
- Session Title
- Description
- ...and possibly Talk Length and Session Type.

Anything further should be asked cautiously - you want to be wary of putting off any new speakers. For example, you may choose to ask if they've spoken before, in order to identify if they need some mentoring, but if that were to make speakers feel that this may be a criteria for selection then they may not submit. You can solve this by simply offering mentoring to anyone who would like it.

Additionally, it could be tempting to ask for a link to a video if they have done the talk before, but this runs the risk of generating a bias towards experienced speakers. Many public conferences will avoid asking this for this very reason - they will even anonymise the submissions when sending them to reviewers in order to minimise this effect.

You may have someone in mind who you think would add a lot of value to the event, in which case now is the time to approach them - encourage them to submit a paper along with everyone else.

2.5.2 Widely promote the CfP

Don't hold back on the noise you create around the launch of the Call for Papers. As Maraney says, *"There are plenty of people in your organisation who have fascinating things to say about their day to day work, but who don't realise that other people will find it interesting. There are also people who have a talk idea, but are nervous about speaking and are waiting to be given a nudge to submit it"* [10]. Now is the time for the big promotional push - get line managers to encourage their team members, put reminders out in management emails and any other comms channels you have, walk up to people who you know have an interesting story and bribe them with cookies and cake, and even do a promotional table in the lunch canteen to capture people's imagination...

2.5.3 Aim for a varied speaker shortlist

When you narrow down the list of potential speakers to a shortlist, you have two choices. Either your organising group can shortlist, based on an agreed set of criteria, or you can put it to a staff vote.

Metaswitch open up the speaker selection to a vote by members of staff, and stick solidly to the result - they feel a fully democratic process is in keeping with the spirit of the event. Klarna have created (and published for transparency) some criteria for scoring talks, and they do this individually first, then collectively (as an organising team) to come up with an agenda they're happy with. (See Chapter 5 more more case study details.)

The third option is a blend of the two. Start with the voting, to establish "the people's choice", but be ready to do some adjustment. Perhaps voting has brought talks that are too similar to the top of the list, perhaps the speakers are non-diverse, or people have voted up mostly extroverted and experienced speakers, or familiar voices from their own teams. There may yet be a particular topic you really want in there to stimulate debate. There is no harm doing a bit of engineering to ensure a healthy mix of sessions.

2.6 Define the schedule

Part of your final speaker selection may come down to the structure of the day and the specific time-slots you have created for them. Now is the time to firm up the schedule. Ask yourself: What time will you start? What time will you finish? How many streams will you have? How many slots will that turn into? Which sessions suit which rooms best (if you have multiple spaces)?

Think about what the mood and energy are like at different times of day. Start with something thoughtful to set the tone of the day. The session immediately after lunch is a good time for something energising as people slow down a little whilst digesting. And finish the day with something lively and memorable.

Remember to allow enough time for tea breaks, for speaker handovers and a decent lunch break. If you are doing something useful with the lunch-break like holding Open Space discussions, then this is not lost time. Plan to use at least 5 minutes per talk for changing over to the next speaker.

Once you have the schedule mapped out, then you can get on with creating your promotional material and getting everyone ready for the day.

2.7 Ensure speakers are ready

It is important to invest time in giving your speakers guidance and support, because ultimately the success of your day depends on them. Begin early with support for speakers, so that they have as much time as possible to prepare.

2.7.1 Prepare some written guides for speakers and contributors

If you are doing an interactive panel discussion, then maintaining a respectful communication style is going to be critical. Consider writing up some guidelines on how to pose challenging questions, and how to respond to direct challenges. An example Panelist Briefing is included in the Toolkit to get you started.

For people giving a talk or presentation, written advice and guidelines on how to structure their talk, how to make the best use of slides, how to move around and even how to breathe (!) can be invaluable. The Toolkit in this book contains some good advice for all speakers, as does the *Doing Presentations* website [56].

2.7.2 Mentor less experienced speakers

Once the guidelines have been shared, make mentors available to new speakers to offer personal experience and advice, listen to practice runs, give feedback on slides, etc. Consider running group practice sessions where people can offer feedback to each other too - this might take some of the fear out of it for new speakers [16].

> The Klarna team considers their speaker mentoring activities a key ingredient in the success of their conferences. See Chapter 5 for details.

2.7.3 Collect speaker biographies

Each speaker will need to provide a short biography (a few sentences or 2-3 paragraphs). This is an opportunity for speakers to think about their "personal brand". Help them come up with a short biography, including a fetching photo, which can go on the posters and website. They can use this for their public speaking career later! Also at this point, ask them how they'd like to be introduced on the day.

2.7.4 Have back-up speakers

Be prepared for one or two speakers dropping out at short notice (it does happen occasionally - emergencies, illnesses, nerves). It's a very good idea to have a couple of backup talks ready with willing participants who don't mind not getting to speak if disaster doesn't strike.

2.8 Ensure attendees are ready

Much as you need speakers to make the day happen, you also need some attendees! In this section we cover the details of how to attract attendees to the event.

2.8.1 Promotion - make some noise, and make it loud!

Just because the organising committee has been busy for weeks planning the event, don't assume that the rest of the department has noticed! With the speaker lineup chosen, now is the time to get the message out and generate some buzz.

This means plenty of printed posters, plenty of email and chat announcements , and generally lots of talking about it whenever possible. The organising team can lead this activity in force - visit team stand-ups, put lots of messages in the team chat systems, take over the big screens around the department. Consider walking around the building with a giant wearable sign! Simply put, make it impossible for people to not know what's happening.

The Metaswitch tactic of getting people to reserve their seat in particular conference sessions could help here, as the "first-come, first-served" nature of seat reservations adds a bit of extra excitement (see Chapter 5).

This is where support from Senior Management can really help. Senior Management should send encouraging emails and messages not just giving people permission to go along, but saying how much they personally back the event. Apart from anything else, they can encourage a no-meeting day to ensure everyone has the freedom and opportunity to attend.

Make it really easy for people to know what's going on. Put the agenda on the printed posters, make a website or wiki page with the details for each session, put it in people's electronic calendars, and have a dedicated electronic chat facility for open discussion as people get ready for the day, etc.

2.8.2 Make your event inclusive

Many event organisers make the mistake of not considering the needs of a wide enough range of people. There are many different forms of sensory and learning impairments and differences that can usually be easily addressed with enough foresight, but which can make it difficult for some people to attend or enjoy an event. The best way to ensure you do enough to include people who need some special consideration (without making unnecessary compromises) is to give attendees the opportunity to tell what they need.

As early as possible - ideally in the initial comms about the event - ask if any attendees (or speakers) need anything to be able to fully participate in the event. This may influence the advice you give to speakers about their presentation materials, or it may influence the layout of the rooms or other services you need to provide. The biggest thing it will achieve is extending that voice out to *all* of your employees and letting them know they matter and will be provided for, thus hopefully encouraging them to join in.

An example of the types of things presenters may need to consider is if you think you are likely to have anyone hard of hearing in attendance, prime your speakers to put more content onto their slides than they otherwise might. Additionally, in order to consider dyslexic attendees and those with eyesight problems, speakers should make their slide text clear and spaced out on a contrasting background - avoiding blurry text over complex images, or tightly crowded lettering [52].

Live captioning is one way to avoid asking your speakers to make compromises on their slide format: the speaker's words are transcribed in real time and displayed as text on a screen for people to read. This excellent service enables you to be as inclusive as possible by allowing your speakers to have highly-engaging slides and for those who struggle to read those to have an alternative. Remember to budget for live captioning if you use it (see the example budget in the Toolkit). There are plenty of detailed and up to date recommendations for slides and talks available online [17].

2.8.3 Insist upon respectful interactions

Given you are hoping this event will stimulate some open and honest communication, it is well worth reminding people of the need to be respectful with it. Your speakers are volunteers, who are bravely putting themselves forward. Questions from the floor are very welcome - but heckling is not. Create a Code of Conduct, and publish it in advance of the event. Make it clear that people violating the Code of Conduct will be asked to leave. There is an example Code of Conduct in the Toolkit later in this book.

2.9 Ensure the space is ready

It is important to prepare the space in which the conference will be held. This section contains advice on choosing and preparing the venue.

2.9.1 Choose and prepare your venue

Ask yourself: *Do you have the facilities in-house to host this event, or do you need to go off-site?*

If you go off-site, then you may find that you get deeper engagement from attendees. By going to the event at all, they are committing to the whole day - and there will definitely be fewer distractions to interrupt the flow. The fact of it being somewhere other than the office can reinforce the message that this is a *different* day to all of the others, and help to shift their mindset.

However, you may not want attendees to feel it's an "all or nothing" choice. Having the ability to go to sessions that appeal to them and dip out of things they're not that interested in retains an element of choice which some may feel is an important part of the day; in such cases, holding the event in the office could be the right option.,

The FT are fortunate enough to have a large conference room in their office and so as long as they plan a single-stream event they can host it there, with very good catering and AV support. Metaswitch, with their multi-stream event, take over every large meeting room in the building - and a local chapel! Their AV tends to be a bit more "home-made", but it also means that the whole building comes alive with the event.

Other companies find the budget to take it off-site altogether. New Relic took this up a big notch in 2018, with a 3-day conference for 500 product and engineering employees in a holiday resort where, amongst typical conference sessions, they had plenty of recreational time for building connections informally. Not many organisations have this sort of budget, but with this investment they are showing just how seriously they take the opportunity to *"think deeply about the future, to run experiments, and to take risks"* [18].

To help you decide what's right for you, consider these things:

2.9.1.1 Budget

What can you afford? Going off-site can be nice but the off-site venue must be a better space than you can provide on-site to lure people away.

There is an example budget later in this book for you to use.

2.9.1.2 Catering options

What sort of space is available for eating and mingling?

What providers are there? Pizzas are popular, but tasty, healthy food is becoming more so as people want something to help their brain focus in the afternoon.

And don't forget all the other dietary considerations - vegan, gluten-free, paleo, allergens, etc. Not everyone drinks alcohol, so have interesting soft drinks.

2.9.1.3 Structure of the day

What structure have you planned? How many spaces do you need concurrently?

2.9.1.4 Ease of travel

You know that everyone can reach your office... Is going-off site just as easy for them, or might you alienate some people?

2.9.1.5 Facilities

Sometimes being in a "quirky" venue can be great for shifting the mind to a more creative space, but if you are in need of projectors and good AV, etc - which we recommend you are - then look for somewhere more practiced at hosting these sorts of events.

2.9.1.6 Accessibility

Remember to factor in the results of having asked people what they need to enable them to fully participate in the day. Do you need space - or even ramps - for wheelchairs? Do you need extra seats for BSL (British Sign Language) interpreters? It's also a good idea to reserve a couple of seats at the front or back of rooms for people who need them most - eg pregnant women, people with back problems.

2.9.1.7 Keep the lights on and maintain service

One more thing to consider if you choose to hold your event off-site, is what that means for business continuity. You are, afterall, proposing to take your entire IT department out of the building! Rich Haigh at Paddy Power Betfair found that *"The biggest problem was that I was intending to take a large number of the tech staff out of the business for a day. In order to mitigate this, we always set up a war-room"* [11].

2.9.2 Provide swag

People like free stuff (swag). There are people who will turn up to any event just for a tasty cupcake. Consider tote bags, coffee cups, notebooks, pens, stickers, etc - the options are only limited to your imagination. These will not only act as a nice reminder later on of the event (except the cupcakes, perhaps), but the swag desk will also provide a handy muster point where organisers can engage with attendees to get some on-the-spot feedback on how the day is going for them.

2.9.2.1 Be cautious with clothing as swag

Custom t-shirts can be great giveaways, and it can be especially useful for the organising team to wear them on the day to make them recognisable, but there is a lot to consider here. Be aware of the sizing options (particularly what "unisex" really means), the cut, and making them attractive enough that people will want to wear them many times [10].

2.9.3 Provide quality catering

Linda Rising, thought leader amongst change agents, says "Do food" if you want people to commune. *"Research shows that we become fonder of people and things we experience while we are eating"*, she says. She goes on to cite research that shows that *"Sharing food plays a vital role in almost all human societies to bind people together and increase the feeling of group membership"* [19]. There's something deeply levelling about chatting over food. It's even better if you bring "good" food - something that says "we made this for you" goes down a lot better than "we got these pizzas on a half-price deal".

Welcome people at the start of the day with some breakfast or other appetizer, then give them plenty to drink and snack on during breaks and a good quality, healthy lunch. Cheap sandwiches are definitely a false economy, as people will spend valuable energy grumbling about those rather than attending to what's going on.

2.9.4 Provide good quality AV and WiFi

You need to make sure you have good quality Audio Visual (AV) and WiFi in place. It takes a highly seasoned speaker to ride out a failure in this equipment, so minimise disruption to a carefully structured day by making sure this is as reliable as you can.

You may be working in a professional AV setup and have people on hand to help with this, including filming and photography. If not, then make sure you have volunteers ready to set things up in each room, including helping people test their connections and troubleshoot any problems.

Make sure speakers are familiar with the AV set-up they'll be expected to use. There will be practicalities to consider in terms of what kind of mic they'll be using, whether they might be playing a video with sound (does their laptop connect to a speaker?) and having a slide clicker that works on their machine.

Soft-covered throwable microphones like the CatchBox speed up the Q&A session. Image credit: Matthew Skelton

2.9.5 Plan for remote access

If your organisation is distributed, then consider what level of involvement you want from smaller off-site teams. There are a variety of options to consider, depending on your budget, the complexity of your set-up and the quality of your facilities.

Metaswitch flew people in from their European offices to maximise the "in-room" experience and shared recordings afterwards with team members in remote offices.

The FT sought input in terms of what topics and questions would be asked, but on the day itself it was a one-way broadcast from the main office. For remote regions they put up local posters, provided local pizza and live streamed YouTube content.

If you do decide to make the conference available to people outside the building, then you will need to ensure that all of your sessions are streamed with high quality audio and video. You should also provide some mechanism through which they can ask questions. This could be an online Q&A tool which collates questions for people to see and upvote, or it could simply be a team chat channel where people type their questions and an in-room representative asks on their behalf.

REMOTE PARTICIPANTS - MAKING IT WORK

Sometimes, it's a good option to include some people at remote locations via video link. Making remote partici-pants feel welcome and part of the event requires some extra effort.

Promotion

Enlist some local champions who will help put up posters (and who will advise on local time adjustments when building the agenda/schedule!).

Physical space

Does the remote region have a big room with a large screen and speakers so that the conference can be broadcast to a room where they can also have a communal experience?

Catering

If you're providing some catering for attendees, consider providing some in remote regions too, so that they can feel fully included in the day.

Be realistic - and test

Despite network improvements in recent years, latency and drop-outs in connectivity are still common. If the network connectivity is not good enough for remote attendees to join in, then resign yourself to sharing videos afterwards. Consider options for helping a remote office to run their own sessions and film them for sharing later.

2.10 Chapter Review

Every event is different, and the types and level of planning will be unique to your context. Use the ideas here to help you build your own plan.

Sort out the basics first:

- Get management buy-in - budget *and* explicit support
- Date - set some deadlines and get focus
- Form a strong team to organise it

Ask yourself: What does management need to know so that they can support the event? And who should be on the organising team?

Choose formats that will meet your objectives:

- Panel discussions to provoke debate
- Talks to inspire
- Workshops for hands-on learning

Ask yourself: What mix of formats will work best?

Your speakers are key to your success:

- Encourage everyone to submit - but don't be scared of a little social engineering
- Be open to a variety of topics, including fun pet projects
- Support your speakers as much as you possibly can

Ask yourself: How heavily do you want to curate your content? Will you trust staff voting, or do you want to choose?

Planning is key to the success of your event:

- Venue selection and layout
- Remote access
- Catering
- *See also the Toolkit later in this book for some guides*

Ask yourself: What other things will you need to consider when planning your event?

Don't be shy when promoting the event:

- Posters
- Website
- Chat channels

Ask yourself: What would make it impossible for people to *not* get excited?

3. Running the conference

This chapter will help you to answer these questions:

- What should we expect on the day?
- Who do we need extra help from on the day?
- What are the potential pitfalls?
- What extra things should we be doing?

3.1 Volunteer army

Having done all the preparation, on the day itself you just need to keep an eye on things to make sure all goes to plan - or that the team adapts well if and when something deviates from the plan. The most important thing is to have your small army of volunteers in place so that you can deal with any problems. Ensure that the volunteers understand the purpose and outcomes for the event, then trust them to make it happen.

3.2 Communicate any late schedule changes

Speakers can fall ill or have a sudden urgent appointment at the hospital or home, so sometimes it is necessary to make last-minute changes to the schedule. Make sure to communicate this clearly to attendees and speakers during the day. You may need to make several announcements to ensure everyone has heard.

If a major event occurs during the day - such as fire alarm - that removes a significant part of the available time, you have two main options:

1. Ask speakers to do a shorter version of their talk. This can be very difficult for some speakers if they have practised their talk.
2. Remove some of the talks from the schedule and agree to video these talks at a later date (perhaps at an internal team session).

Of course, if attendees are happy to stay longer - and if you have access to the venue - you could continue with the original set of talks, but beware that some people may need to leave, and you may lose the sense of togetherness from having everyone experience the same set of talks.

3.3 Make it easy to attend the right sessions

Provide attendees and speakers with a variety of ways to navigate the venue and the sessions. A combination of printed schedules, online schedules, and a schedule via email works well. You could also provide a venue map showing the different rooms and location of toilets, food, quiet rooms, etc. Prominently position a large sign outside each room with its name and the list of sessions scheduled to be held in it so that people can be certain that they have found the right room. Provide direction signs around the venue if the venue is large or confusing ("This way to the main hall →" and so on).

3.4 Make speakers finish on time

It is essential to maintain good timekeeping throughout the day. If every talk overruns by 5 minutes, you can easily lose space for an entire talk later in the day. After the speaker has had their 15, 10 and 5-minute warnings, the time-keeper should be ready to tell the speaker to "finish quickly, please" or similar. It is usually clear if the speaker is not close to finishing. If in doubt, and if the speaker has used up all the allotted time, simply say "thank you, but we will have to leave it there as we have run out of time". Make sure the speaker gets a round of applause and thank them for their talk, but do not let them continue speaking after their allotted time.

It is usually good to have 5 or 10 minutes for questions after a talk, so plan for this time in your talk schedule: a 30 minute slot is really a 20-minute talk with 5 minutes of questions and 2 minutes of setting up at the beginning and end of the talk.

3.5 Make speakers use a microphone

Insist that every speaker and panellist uses a microphone: no excuses and no exceptions. Speaking is not a macho competition to project your voice to the back of the room. Microphones improve the experience for everyone, including people with hearing loss and for the video. In doing so, make sure you think about the questions from the audience - the mic used by the speaker won't pick those up for the video (whether it's live-streamed or simply recorded for posterity). Either have extra microphones that are connected to the video, or ask your speakers to repeat all questions before answering.

Good quality audio is essential for both speakers and audience. Image credit: Matthew Skelton

3.6 Cover all operational aspects

There are many things that need to happen simultaneously during the conference day itself. You will need to have various people playing specific roles. We suggest you recruit volunteers to adopt some or most of the roles below to ensure smooth running during the day.

3.6.1 Host / Compere / MC

Who is going to be the host for the day? Someone needs to welcome everyone, introduce and thank each speaker, remind attendees to give feedback, and wrap up the day with directions to the evening social event. The host should also ensure that speakers have water and power for their laptops.

3.6.2 Registration

If you want to register attendees, you will need people ready to welcome them and sign them in and hang out swag and gifts. Identify your back-up speakers and make sure they are prepared to step in if needed.

3.6.3 Ushers

Have people ready to spot and greet speakers and get them poised ready to go up at the right time. Ushers can also be great for encouraging people to take their seats so that talks get started promptly. It's also a good idea to have the ushers congratulate the speakers as soon as they leave the stage.

3.6.4 AV support

Each room needs someone helping with Audio-Visual, ensuring the transition between speakers goes smoothly (including ensuring people have clip-mics switched *off* if they go for a last minute bathroom visit before going on stage!).

Ideally, AV support will help speakers test things early, so these volunteers should be in place an hour before the conference is due to start to catch those who are super-prepared.

3.6.5 Photographer

Someone should be taking stylish photos to capture the spirit of the day for using in follow-ups. Use a good SLR camera rather than just a smartphone.

Don't forget to warn people that photos will be taken and give them the opportunity to opt out of being in any photos that get used later.

3.6.6 Chat channel watcher

It's recommended that you have an open chat channel in whatever team chat system you use, for people to ask questions or raise problems. Someone should be watching that and ready to tackle whatever comes up.

3.6.7 Communications

Having someone ready to post out corrections or updates into the chat channel and the website - and even with post-it sticky notes on posters if need be - can make sure people are kept informed of any changes that happen to the schedule. Those can be planned changes - like urls to the live streamed talks being posted once they're created - or they could be unplanned, like a change in speaker.

3.6.8 Plants in the audience

Consider having one or two 'plants' in the audience: people who are primed with interesting questions. People can be shy and find it hard to be the first to ask a question. On top of that, it can take a moment to absorb what they've been listening to and formulate questions, as well as planning how to articulate this without stuttering or tripping up verbally. Having a confident ally planted ready to ask a worthwhile question can really help others to ask questions too.

3.6.9 Journalists

Have a couple of people capturing highlights from talks, ready to use in post-event blogs and write-ups. Even people who have been in a talk can enjoy someone else's summary, and for those who were unable to make it this is a nice quick way for them to catch up on what they missed.

3.6.10 Time-keepers

Keeping the talks on-time is an important job. Have someone at the back of each room, with signs to hold up to show speakers when they have 15, 10, 5 and 0 minutes left. This will help speakers a huge amount!

3.6.11 Microphone runners

When questions are being asked from the floor, it's best to try and catch them on a microphone so that they get captured on the video recording. Having mic runners just helps this remain co-ordinated.

3.7 Enhance attendee experience

There are a few extra touches you could consider on the day to make the experience as good as possible for attendees:

3.7.1 Music

Consider some theme music to play at the start and then between sessions. This can be a useful tool not just for adding punctuation, but also for raising the energy levels of the day.

3.7.2 Feedback forms

Provide printed feedback forms for people to fill in immediately after a talk finishes. Many people like to give feedback right away, so printed sheets can make them feel that their views are being heard. Specific actionable comments are by far the most valuable kind of feedback.

3.7.3 Quiet Room

Some people can become rather overwhelmed at events with many hundreds of people, even if these people are colleagues. A Quiet Room can be a good place for these people to "decompress" and de-stress in between talks. There should be no talking in the Quiet Room, no digital noises (from phones or computers), and the lighting should be dimmed.

3.7.4 Realtime retrospective

Provide a space for people to put up remarks about things that are going well (or not). Emily Webber's experiences at public events with these "realtime retrospectives" are convincing [51] - this type of board makes it incredibly easy for participants to drip-feed their thoughts as and when they have them.

It can give a speaker a real boost to see them highlighted on the realtime retrospective board, and also it can give volunteers who are running the day an opportunity to learn early if something's not working so they can respond. The more general feedback is great material for when you reflect on the day later to learn from the experience.

See the Toolkit later in this book for details of how to use a Realtime Retrospective.

3.8 Chapter Review

Use the ideas here to help you have a smooth-running event.

You'll need a team of extra volunteers on the day:

- Photographers and journalists to capture the day
- AV support to ensure the equipment works well
- Timekeepers to make sure people finish their talks promptly

Ask yourself: Who else do you need to have in place to ensure everything you have planned works as intended?

Be aware of possible problems, and be ready to adapt:

- Have back-up speakers prepared
- Be ready to flex times/slots if needed
- Prepare for problems with video & audio for remote participants

Ask yourself: What parts of the day are you most nervous about? Do you have contingencies in place, or people looking out for those things and ready to handle them?

Some extra touches you might add to the day:

- A theme tune for the day, to keep the energy high
- A quiet room for people to decompress
- Realtime retrospective to capture immediate feedback

Ask yourself: What "little extras" could help make your event memorable and unique?

4. Follow-up

This chapter will help you to answer these questions:

- How will I know if this has been a successful event?
- How do I stop people from forgetting about it?
- How do I maximise the results?

4.1 Gather feedback

Use printed or digital feedback forms to ask people what they hoped they'd get from the day, and whether it was successful. What did they enjoy, or not enjoy? What do they think went well, and what could be improved next time? Hopefully they won't just talk about there not being enough pizza because naturally you'll have provided some quality catering as per this book's recommendations.

It will be useful for you to ask that same question of those people who spoke or debated at this year's events too so that you know how to improve things for speakers next year.

Also ask at this point what they intend to do next as a result of the conference - simply asking this question might prompt them to think about it, and be more likely to take action as a result. Ask if they'd be willing to participate in some way next time - perhaps point this question at people who felt braver contributing from the floor, to assess if this event has given them some confidence in their views.

4.2 Reflect, then follow-through

As with anything else you try to achieve as a team in a modern agile organisation, it is important for the organising team to stop and reflect. Review the feedback you've received and ask yourselves these questions:

- *Did this conference achieve what we wanted it to? How do we know?*
- *What should we do differently next time to make it more effective?*
- *What went really well this time that we want to make sure we remember to do next time?*
- *What needs to happen now to make sure the good things that came out of it are sustainable?*

When you've reflected, share your observations with the senior leadership team - particularly your views on sustaining the changes. Whilst a major reason for holding an internal tech conference is to give ordinary people a voice and widen the conversation within the organisation, the leadership team still has a big role to play in ensuring that the conversation continues afterwards.

4.2.1 Revisit your anticipated benefits

In Chapter 1 you identified some expected benefits from running an internal tech conference. Now is the time to consider how well the event met these goals.

4.2.1.1 Celebrate your unsung heroes - don't stop now!

Having given the unsung heroes of the organisation a chance to shine during the conference, you can now celebrate them and their work throughout the year. Reinforce the message presented by the speakers by using it for some ongoing communications to remind people of the good work happening. Feature the speakers in departmental newsletters, award recognition for achieving an improvement in service or resilience, and so on.

4.2.1.2 Release your speakers into the wild

Many speakers talk about the huge emotional hurdle they had to overcome to do their first talk at an internal tech conference. Perhaps they will now have the confidence to take their talk outside to a public conference - all the benefits they gained from giving an internal talk will be even greater when given externally. They will find networking easier when they've given a talk: people will want to talk to them about their chosen topic. It's great for you as an organisation to have people at public events contributing to the community, and it's great for them as speakers to get some exposure and to connect with other people who can help them learn more.

Support them in becoming ambassadors for your organisation at meetups and conferences. The Financial Times created a Speakers Guild, which enables some swapping of good practise ideas, and a safe space for new speakers to practice in, which has dramatically increased the number of people willing to go out into the industry to talk (see Chapter 5).

4.2.1.3 Help cross-team learning to continue

Look for any signs of people wanting to stimulate further connections and contextual learning, such as Hack Days, guilds, Communities of Practice, bootcamps, or peer-training sessions. A simple but concrete thing you can do to support and encourage employee-led activities like this is to provide some food and drink to accompany promising-looking activities. It will help to reinforce the sense of being valued and invested in, without taking anything away from the employees who are setting things in motion. Promoting these activities in your departmental newsletter and other channels will show management support and give recognition to those who are stepping forward to contribute.

With luck, you will see follow-ups instigated by employees, but an occasional "nudge" from a supportive leadership team will help to ensure the space and encouragement is there to see the true value of your event be fulfilled in the longer term.

You can also ask people who submitted talks to the conference but who were not selected to give their talks at tech-talks/brown bag sessions during the year.

4.2.2 Say "thank you"

Make sure you send out a big newsletter at the end of your conference. Offer lots of thanks for all those hard-working volunteers who helped bring it together and share some headlines and videos to remind people of some of the best moments of the day. Consider giving small gifts to speakers.

Finally, write up a summary of the day on a public tech blog. It acts as a great reminder to those who are tempted to quickly forget the event!

4.3 Chapter Review

Hopefully your conference has gone well and a good time was had by all. Use the ideas here to help you learn as much as you can from the experience, and to get the most value out of your investment in this event.

Were your objectives met? Do your attendees agree?

- Get feedback from attendees and participants to ensure they got what they wanted from the event, and to make next time even better.
- Reflect on your goals and consider the evidence - now and later

Ask yourself: What evidence did you see on the day of people's engagement levels? What further evidence of event outcomes do you need to look for?

Make sure people have a lasting memory of this event:

- Internal blog post with photos and highlights
- Internal newsletter with lots of thanks
- External blog post to celebrate

Ask yourself: What specific communication media are available to you to capture and share the event activities afterwards?

It doesn't stop here - the best bits come afterwards:

- Notice and encourage spin-off groups acting on ideas from the event

- Encourage speakers to go externally and become ambassadors

Ask yourself: What other activities or events can you do throughout the year to build on this event?

5. Case studies

This chapter consists of case studies from three organisations:

- The Financial Times (FT)
- Metaswitch
- Klarna

5.1 Case study: The Financial Times

The Financial Times is one of the world's leading news organisations, recognised internationally for its authority, integrity and accuracy. It is part of Nikkei Inc., which provides a broad range of information, news and services for the global business community.

The story of the FT's experience of internal conferences is deeply fascinating. Internal conferences offer a window into what is happening within the broader Product & Technology department and provide opportunities to communicate any changes within the team.

During the four years covered in this case study, the FT saw three things emerge:

A dramatic growth in pride and recognition of product and technical excellence

Showcasing innovation and letting people tell their stories at these events all encouraged more experiments and boundary-pushing by teams afterwards.

Enabling the sharing of pain points across teams galvanised people to break out of their silos and find creative and tangible solutions to problems.

Dedicating time to talking about what their engineers were proud of triggered a new passion for setting and raising the standards, for inspiring each other and generating excitement that was longer lasting.

Open debates brought Product and Technology together to form a powerful partnership. Previously two separate groups, the Product and Technology departments came to recognise each other and ultimately combine in 2016 - leading to far smarter decisions being made around their business model and tech strategies.

The conference was a manifestation of cultural change and then a yardstick for measuring it

The department saw *emergent leadership;* opening up the floor to questions and topics encouraged new voices.

Open debates and the freedom to discuss topics led to the evolution of a *deep democracy* for some difficult departmental changes such as adopting DevOps and shifting ownership for Quality Assurance to engineers.

The *bonding experience* of the event created connections that continued far beyond the day - peer coaching and training activities were spun up and a new rhythm of bootcamps and rotations between teams helped conversations to continue.

The FT became a destination employer - a place people wanted to be

Everyone started to take responsibility for making the FT somewhere they wanted to be, no longer relying on the leadership team to set the rules.

More people started talking about diversity & inclusion, psychological safety, empathy and respect. Employee-led initiatives and groups started to form around mental health, diversity, coaching and mentoring, in addition to various engineering specialisms.

Engineers started to contribute to the wider community, such as engaging with coding clubs for under-represented groups outside the organisation, talking at conferences about what they do and providing open-source toolkits for building accessible websites.

"Nudge"

An internal tech conference cannot possibly take all the credit for a cultural transformation, but it can play a big part and mark out a useful rhythm of checkpoints.

Thaler and Sunstein coined the term *Libertarian Paternalism* in their book *Nudge - Improving decisions about health, wealth and happiness* [20]. It refers to the desire to give people the freedom of choice whilst also keeping an eye on what is good for the person. It means creating opportunities for people to make decisions - and making it easy for them to make the decision that is in their best interests, without removing their right to make a "bad" decision.

So all these activities - inspiring a forum where conversations that are happening in small pockets could reach a wider audience for debate, and then gently encouraging some of the spin-off activities it triggered - could be viewed as simply a series of nudges. Neither the conference, nor its agenda, nor even the follow-up activities were created by the leadership team but were merely the conditions for them to happen.

5.1.1 How it all began

Unwittingly, the FT triggered their first event just as a cultural shift was trying to happen - so what started out as a conference about technology became a catalyst for real change.

That change can be mapped out across the next four years - each conference not only nudging that transformation along a bit, but also acting as a mirror to reflect on just how far the department's culture had evolved since the previous event.

The decision to run the event came the day after some engineers and their CTO attended a large external conference. This group realised that the recent changes that had already happened at the FT - a massive growth in investment in technology, accompanied by a broad move towards agility in terms of methods, processes, engineering practices and technology choices - meant there was a huge amount of knowledge and experience within the department already. The challenge at that time was not a lack of knowledge, but a lack of *knowledge-share.*

Much has been said about the challenges of empowered teams and about the silos that happen as a direct result of team autonomy. Independent structures are great for streamlined decision-making and agility, but dreadful in terms of sharing ideas, services, skills, experiences and best practices.

Not only that, but there were an awful lot of *opinions* that weren't being shared. Leadership would talk about agility, about empowerment, about wanting a collaborative culture - but if they were the only ones doing the talking, then change was going to be very slow indeed.

The decision was made: run an internal technical conference, "by the people, for the people". This would mean a group of volunteers from within the department creating it from scratch, calling upon their colleagues to generate content.

5.1.2 2015 - it began with a vision

Over the past few years there has been an almost exponential increase in the speed of change within the technology sphere. Coupled with this has been the growth of the FT Technology department in terms of numbers and expertise. The size, scope and speed of delivery is greater than ever. It is close to impossible for individuals to keep abreast of all these changes.

However, communication, in a friendly, inclusive environment, can help. By communicating we can address the challenges and increase the benefits of this rapid change. We can and should learn from each other so that great ideas, useful tools and smart ways of working can be shared.

Vision statement:

- **Engine Room Live** is an internal conference for the FT Technology department, an opportunity to learn from each other and make connections between teams to increase communication, productivity and innovation.
- **Participants** get a chance to take part in a conversation that matters to them, and to test out their public speaking voice in a safe environment.
- **Attendees** get to discover and take away good ideas and new channels of communication with other attendees. A chance to lift your head from the weeds and think about something other than delivering the next feature.
- **The company** gets better working practices spread around more teams, happier staff and improved communication between teams and people, so that job satisfaction, productivity and efficiency can increase.

They sold it to the rest of the department as a chance to 'lift your heads up from the coal face for a day and maybe even choose a better pickaxe' [40].

FT's tech department leaders showed their support for the event by joining in as delegates on the day. The department's Delivery Coach kicked things off with a short introductory talk on how much the FT Technology department had changed in the last few years and how a conference fitted in perfectly with the 'always learning' ethos of the FT's then parent company Pearson [22].

Having set the scene, a day of panel discussions followed - some of which were written up enthusiastically by attendees on the FT's blog [23]. Having invested a lot of energy and excitement into the day, the results were remarkable.

Questions during panel discussion at FT. Image credit: Michal Huniewicz

No-one quite anticipated just how much impact the day could have. Here is what emerged:

- Teams came away saying they would definitely be trying new ways of working (the organisers followed up - they did!).
- A monitoring "action group" emerged as a result of opening up a discussion on dealing with alerting overload in the world of microservices - one team's problem became a department-wide challenge to focus on.
- A centralised Dev Tooling team, who owned the automated deployment mechanisms, committed publicly to making small individual tools for dev teams to free them from the perceived tyranny of central control.

Most importantly, there was a real sense that people had started to think about how they could change things. The event itself - and the CTO's talk at the end of the day about how people needed to take empowerment, rather than waiting for it to be bestowed upon them - had a profound effect and encouraged lots of opinion-sharing over the drinks that followed that evening. Those opinions continued to be shared and debated over the next few weeks and months.

5.1.3 2016 - change is in the air

By the time the second conference came around in 2016, a lot had changed already, and 25 people volunteered to help organise it. More topics were put forward for discussion, more people volunteered to sit on the panels - people had found their voices! People who had sat on panels in the first year were now speaking at external conferences; other people who had been inspired to realise they could *make change happen* had begun lunchtime learning sessions and working groups.

Some of the attendees in 2016 felt that they'd been a bit shy the first time around, and wanted to get stuck into the *really hard* topics this year. So DevOps got some real attention - *with one of the most brave, respectful, but deeply honest discussions that could be hoped for with a topic that impacted so many people across the technology department.*

It was obvious at this point that the FT's Tech and Product team no longer relied on their leadership team to talk about change - movements were beginning from the ground up and they were starting to see employee-led change.

5.1.4 2017 - getting into the groove

Fast-forward to 2017, and the topics that were being discussed had moved from technical challenges to cultural issues. Diversity and Inclusion featured highly and some very candid, sometimes painful stories were told to a room full of 150 colleagues - a moment that made FT Technology leadership proud. It legitimized the claim that the FT Product & Technology team has a great culture of respect, openness and honesty.

If it is not already clear - *internal tech conferences are about so much more than tech.*

5.1.5 2018 - change is Business As Usual

By 2018, conversations about the type of organisation the FT wants to be were a part of the fabric. There were year-round employee-led working groups on diversity and inclusion, leadership skills, collaboration styles, accessibility, standards, data and success metrics. People were now familiar with the idea that if they wanted something to change, they could start the conversation.

In terms of public speaking experiences, there were regular Lightning Talk sessions to give people a small non-threatening window to speak at, social events organised by a "Culture Club" and lots of "pop-up" (*ad hoc*) learning activities.

5.1.5.1 Pushing the boundaries

A major change in the preceding 12 months was the opportunity for further collaboration across the FT and with external organisations. The company had been bought by Nikkei in 2016 [24], and so the FT team had been involved in collaborations with the Nikkei technology department; they also worked on an innovative external project with Google. Partner companies were also now working with the FT to build capabilities for their "FT Specialist" publications.

5.1.5.2 A new type of conference

The focus of 2018's Engine Room conference was on helping people within the department to lift their head up and realise that whilst cross-team collaboration is amazing, *cross-organisation* collaboration is even more so! The main organiser said he wanted to *"help people understand that we're a bigger organisation than they think"* [25].

With a different purpose comes a different format. This was more of a top-down piece of education for the department, and partners were brought in to share their knowledge, creating an opportunity for awareness and cross-fertilisation of ideas at a broader level. A fixed agenda of well-attended talks with Q&A time replaced the panel sessions of previous years.

So many of the important conversations about how people work together - working styles, technology choices and coming together to solve bigger issues - now just happen because the channels for discourse are open and well used.

5.1.6 What's next for Engine Room Live?

The FT will bring back panel sessions in 2019, where the original values and vision of Engine Room Live will be revisited.

The values of the first conference - "by the people for the people", building up social capital by opening up debates and letting the audience dictate the conversation - have become deeply embedded in the organisation. They didn't *need* a big event to bring this to life in 2018, but they're not ready to take them for granted just yet either!

5.1.7 3 Takeaways

Across FT's four years of Engine Room conferences, some high level lessons are:

There is so much more to a tech conference than tech

This could be your chance to engage your department in some powerful conversations so that they can help define and shape the way forward.

It doesn't stop at the event itself

If you are clear on your objectives, they should continue to be pursued outside of the event. Follow up to ensure that there is an immediate impact, but also be ready to nudge and nurture other complementary activities in pursuit of your goals.

Always focus on what you are trying to achieve when deciding on your format

As your department changes, so will your needs from an event such as this. Don't be afraid to change a tried and tested formula if your needs have evolved.

5.2 Case study: Metaswitch

Metaswitch is a "software for telecommunications" company with 800-900 people worldwide. Whilst most of the technology teams work in the UK, some are across Europe, the US, New Zealand and Malaysia.

For Metaswitch, the motivation for running an annual internal tech conference is pretty simple; it's to keep engineers energised, engaged and innovative. Other departments within the organisation started the trend of annual events by running global training days, flying teams in from around the world to offer a consistent and shared educational experience. Being less globally distributed than the other parts of their organisation, the technology department did not have the same motivations, but it inspired them to consider what they could achieve themselves if they got everyone together in engineering for a couple of days.

This led to them holding their first technical conference to see if people liked it – which they did. Calum Loudon (Lead Architect and conference organiser) tells us that whilst the benefit for the sales team of a day together was formal and consistent training, for the technology department it was all about cohesion and the chance to educate, learn from and inspire their peers.

The developers at Metaswitch say that *the reason they work there is the calibre of their fellow developers* - so this is what they want to highlight with their conference.

They've been running events for five years, and have a consistent format and method that "feels really grooved now", says Loudon. (See the Toolkit in this book for some helpful tools for getting your own conference to run smoothly.)

Several weeks before the event they start to drum-up interest and launch a Call for Papers (with an incredible **80** submissions, interest in the 2018 event was clear long before they even got to the day.). The final list of talks is selected by the votes of the attendees, with some minor tweaks to avoid giving individuals multiple appearances and to fit the schedule into the various rooms that have been co-opted for the event (including the neighbouring church hall!).

Metaswitch have identified that people can need "strong encouragement" to lift themselves out of the day-to-day engineering and development routine, so they explicitly ask everyone to attend. Limited capacity for many talks means that places must be booked in advance, which in itself can set the office abuzz. Within minutes of the announcement inviting people to register their interest, tools are collectively downed as people race to get a seat in their favourite sessions.

Whether it is the strong encouragement to attend, the limited seats in talks, the parties and games held afterwards, or the wide variety of talks (anything from "How I built a grandfather clock out of LEGO" to "Diversity in the workplace", with lots ot engineering and science-related talks in between), their annual event now has a strong reputation within the organisation.

5.2.1 Making people feel valued

Metaswitch have found that investing in their people in this way sustains a high level of morale and engagement in the organisation. Post-conference surveys record consistently high satisfaction, with over 95% of participants reporting positive views on the conference, and with many comments singling out the quality of co-workers as the key highlight [3]. The enthusiasm with which the Call for Papers is met means the reputation of the events is clearly sustained from year to year.

The Metaswitch goal of sustaining a high level of engagement is not only pursued within the conference - they hold twice-yearly hackathons [26] and other social events too. Many staff tell them this event is a highlight of their year.

5.2.2 Side-effects

Whilst keeping people engaged and fresh is the goal of the event, when asked if Metaswitch had seen anything else change, Loudon identified two things:

> At the last Eng Conference we had a session on "I am an X", where various people stood up and related their experience of working at Metaswitch as a woman/trans/non-binary/carer, etc. That I think helped advance a discussion we had been having and led (albeit indirectly) to various initiatives on team cultures and psychological safety.
>
> More generally: a significant part of my day job as head of our architecture team is spotting when different teams are addressing similar problems and getting them to talk to each other. I have

noticed that since we started running Engineering Conferences teams are better at doing that for themselves, i.e. they are less insular and more prone to asking themselves "Hang on, has anyone else solved this problem already?" rather than doing the traditional heads-down engineer thing of rushing off and building it themselves.

5.2.3 3 Takeaways

There are 3 core threads running through all of the Metaswitch Engineering Conferences which are key to their success:

Let the people choose

Don't equate internal conferences with education - this is about celebrating your people. This means that (just like Hackathons) the most successful conferences can come out of being completely open to any type of content - resist the urge to push a particular agenda if you want high engagement. Hopefully you should get some wonderful surprises and uncover creativity in places you would never think to look.

Encourage contribution from all

Your attendees are not just looking for those people who already talk actively at conferences and who will give a polished performance - they are looking for a good story. They're also looking for a reason to stand up and talk next year, so make sure that when shortlisting you select a variety of speakers to encourage less confident speakers to join in.

Don't forget the fun

All the best conferences "out there" include a party or dinner of some kind - this informal part of the event is every bit as important as the conference content. In order to really feel like a treat and a genuine break from work into something different, you need to raise those spirits, encourage those connections and give people something to remember. Some games, prizes, food and drink will give your event a significant boost and maximise the returns you will get from it.

Calum Louden, Lead Architect and conference organiser at Metaswitch

5.3 Case study: Klarna

Founded in 2005 as an e-commerce startup, Klarna is now one of Europe's largest banks and provides payment solutions for 60 million consumers across 100,000 merchants in fourteen countries.

In 2014, Klarna began to run a yearly internal tech conference called *KonferenSE* (a play on the words "Klarna" and Sweden ("SE"), where Klarna is based). A small group of engineers at Klarna realised that an internal tech conference could be a good way to help inspire and educate technology people whilst also providing an occasion for people to network and get to know each other:

> *At Klarna I've found the relationships formed at the KonferenSE valuable throughout the year. Chatting to people between sessions and listening to speakers helps me discover 'local experts' who I can approach for help or advice in their areas of expertise long after the event is over. When I go into a meeting*

about collaboration or integration with a new team the atmosphere is much more friendly (and effective) if I've already had a friendly chat with them at the KonferenSE. - Ben Maraney, organiser

The first few conferences had over 350 participants, with attendance growing in size each year as Klarna expanded. Klarna now employs over 2000 staff; at the 2018 conference nearly 700 staff attended, meaning that nearly all the invited attendees were present.

At a rapidly-growing technology company - especially one with a banking license and with offices in several countries like Klarna - coordinating technical approaches across the organisation becomes increasingly difficult as the company adds more staff. The *KonferenSE* events have evolved over several years to meet this challenge.

5.3.1 Developing speaker skills

One of the most important ingredients of the Klarna conferences has been the focus on developing speaker skills. For the 2018 conference, there were 15 or 16 speaker "mentors" or coaches who worked with people whose talks had been chosen for the conference. Giving a talk at a conference requires skill and practice, and the mentors help the speakers to prepare their material, write the slides, and practice the talk itself. The mentors set deadlines for various draft versions of the talk so that no speaker leaves things until the last minute to prepare.

To help make talks engaging to watch, Klarna pays for professional training for their speakers. The training helps speakers both to prepare the material and to actually give a presentation. In this way, many basic errors of conference talks are avoided: small text on slides, speakers turning away from the audience, speakers mumbling, too much material, and similar problems are caught and avoided early on.

The speakers selected for the upcoming conference act as a little community that help each other to prepare. Speakers are also encouraged to try out their talks with small groups so that problems with the flow of ideas can be found and fixed.

Slides are important. The Klarna mentors help speakers to design slides that look great and are memorable, avoiding bullet points, standard fonts and templates. Good slides actually help the audience to focus on what the speaker is saying, and help (or force) the speaker to memorise their talk rather than read from text on the screen.

The Klarna team found it useful to have a few backup speakers ready to give a talk if one of the scheduled speakers was ill. The backup speaker got all the care and attention that a scheduled speaker got (training, food, swag, and so on) and even if they could not speak on the day, they were selected to give an internal talk soon after the conference.

5.3.2 3 Takeaways

5.3.2.1 Separate the "core organisers" and the "speaker mentors"

"One of the best improvements we made was to have separate people for the core organising (including on-the-day operations) and the speaker mentoring", says Kim Öberg, one of the organising team. The activities and focus for a speaker mentor is quite different from the things that need to happen on the conference day, and keeping these two groups of people separate (to focus on their role) proved to be very valuable.

5.3.2.2 Allow time to prepare for each event

Preparations for a *KonferenSE* event begin 9 months beforehand. Nine months may seem like a long time but it provides plenty of opportunity to mentor and train speakers, prepare talks and slides, and ensure that the conference has a friendly but professional feel. With over 700 attendees, it can be a challenge to find a venue large enough, so early preparation helps. With a growing organisation, the extra time helps the organisers and mentors to consider multiple viewpoints within Engineering, helping to broaden the reach of the event and increase awareness of additional aspects of running a major European banking operation. A good preparation window also enables the organising team to make changes to the event; for example, for the 2019 event, the organising team is considering running dedicated talk tracks with specific themes due to the volume and high quality of the talk submissions.

5.3.2.3 Continuing success

The internal tech conferences at Klarna have been very successful, producing all kinds of advantages that were not initially expected. The Chief Product Officer (CPO) at Klarna, David Fock, is a huge fan of the conference, and gives a 30 minute product vision talk immediately after the morning keynote. The conference is attended by many people outside the technology department, helping to provide cohesion between different parts of Klarna.

Read more about engineering at Klarna: engineering.klarna.com

Ben Maraney, Case Taintor, Kim Öberg, Matthias Feist - current and former organisers of the KonferenSE internal tech conferences at Klarna.

Toolkit for internal tech conferences

This section includes a set of checklists and materials that will help you prepare and run an internal conference. These are suggestions only and are designed to guide you, so feel free to use, change, or discard entirely based upon your own needs.

Building a schedule

Your agenda will vary dramatically depending upon the format of the sessions you decide upon. Here are some tips.

Welcome kick-off

The host/MC should start the day with an early welcome, including a reminder of what's coming up, the structure of the day, and how to interact - either in the room or remotely. Make sure you begin the day at a time that allows all attendees to be present, and allow plenty of time (up to 1 hour) for people to register and collect swag.

Start with an inspirational keynote

Start with someone to set the tone for the day, injecting some early energy to get people ready to positively engage. It needn't be very long - 20 minutes can be quite sufficient. Make sure the topic is something everyone will enjoy.

Have a couple of longer length sessions in the morning

These morning sessions are likely to be the ones where people will have the most energy. Make the most of them by having your more thoughtful sessions here. If you have a mixture of long talks and interactive sessions in your day, you may choose to have your talks in the morning.

A refreshment break is important to give speakers time to switch over, and for people to process the first session before the second one starts.

Have a full lunch break

Ensure you have a full lunch break (at least 45 minutes). It's easy to see the lunch time as "wasted", but this is a false economy for two reasons. First, the lunch break will give people a chance to "recharge" mentally and be ready for the afternoon. Second, the morning should have given people something to think about and discuss with others over food.

Schedule something more lightweight or entertaining immediately after lunch

Immediately after lunch when people are digesting their food is famously a time when energy levels are low. Consider a couple of lightning talks here to invigorate the room. As with the morning, a couple of longer length sessions separated by a coffee break is good.

Finish with something rousing

There is a long tradition of saving the best until last. Consider that a gymnast will always put her most impressive skill at the end of the routine, that fireworks designers put the big burst at the end, and that the fourth movement of the symphony is always the most powerful one. Your internal conference is no different; make your final session a good one - something thought-provoking and memorable! This also encourages people to stay the whole day rather than leaving early [53].

Don't forget to say "Thank you"

The host/MC should conclude the day with plenty of thanks - thank all the participants, all the volunteers and all the attendees who really got stuck in. Summarise the day, covering the key messages of the talks and discussions, issuing a challenge to the attendees to take away whatever they've heard and find their own way to do something useful with it.

Finally, and this is crucial, direct everyone to where they can find the drinks and evening social events.

Example schedule

Here's an example schedule structure:

Time	Room 1	Room 2
09:30	Welcome & breakfast	
10:00	Opening Keynote	
10:30	Thoughtful Talk 1	Hands on with IoT
	Joe Bloggs	Hacker Helen
	(Talk)	(Workshop)
11:15	*Break*	
11:30	Thoughtful Talk 2	Personal Project
	Jane Doe	Practice Pankaj
	(Talk)	(Talk)
12:15	*Lunch*	*Open Spaces*
13:15	Lightning Talks	
14:00	Panel Discussion 1	Life as an x at this company
	Moderator Maria	Speaker x
	4 panelists	(Talk)
	(Panel discussion)	
14:45	*Break*	
15:30	Panel Discussion 2	Rules I'd like to break
	Moderator Mel	Speaker z
	4 panelists	(Goldfish bowl discussion)
	(Panel discussion)	
16:15	*Break*	
16:30	Lightning Talks	
17:00	Closing Keynote	
17:30	Thank you and close	
18:00	Games & Social	

Example checklists

You may decide that it would help your organising team to take individual responsibility for certain areas in order to keep track of things, in which case splitting your tasks/checklists out into categories like this might be a good idea.

These are all merely suggested timeframes and tasks - you should devise your own, but these will hopefully help you to get started.

Initiation

Before the event planning can begin, there are some fundamentals you need to get in place.

Timeline	Activity
12 weeks to go	Vision and format decided
	Management support and budget obtained
	Organising team formed
	Date selected
	Venue selected and booked
4 weeks to go	Volunteers recruited for activities that need them on the day

Speakers

Your speakers are key, and need much attention. Make them feel supported in any way you can - these are just some of the specific tasks involved in that. You may also wish to include the occasional cup of coffee.

Timeline	Activity
11 weeks to go	Desirable speakers approached (internal & external) Call for Papers launched
9 weeks to go	Call for Papers closed and voting open Speaker training prepared - materials, practice opportunities, community, etc.
8 weeks to go	Speakers & sessions selected: - Non-selected speakers let down gently - Selected speakers committed - Back-up speakers identified and included in all prep ongoing
7 weeks to go	Speaker training held Logistics sorted out for external speakers, e.g. travel, who will receive them, perhaps a lunchtime meet & greet slot for attendees to meet them
5 weeks to go	Speakers submitted short Bio, photo and Session Title
4 weeks to go	Speakers submitted Session Synopsis for the website
3 weeks to go	Speakers doing lots of practice dry-runs of their talks Slides shared with organising team for feedback: - Are they the right ratio for the projector/screen? - Is the colour balance right for the light levels in the rooms?

Promotion

Promotion of the internal tech conference is a crucial aspect of its success. To help with this, see the example promotion plan later in this Toolkit.

Agenda

Get your agenda locked down as early as you can - but do it collaboratively. It's important your speakers feel they have a say in where/when they will be talking if at all possible.

Remember when putting this together to make sure that the rooms you are putting sessions into are the right "fit". Make sure you try and visualise the session before committing it to the agenda. Printing out the session titles on paper and moving them around on a table may help.

Timeline	Activity
7 weeks to go	Speakers, sessions and time-slots identified Basic agenda reviewed and approved/committed to by speakers High level structure published on website and posters
4 weeks to go	Detailed programme updated on website, with Session Synopsis, Speaker Bios and Photos

Sessions

Each session should have these things checked off:

Timeline	Activity
4 weeks to go	Specific requirements for room layout confirmed AV needs identified Session registration launched (if you have limited spaces and want people to register)
3 weeks to go	AV arranged - whether this is professional or volunteers Session run-throughs done
1 week to go	Slide deck complete

Timeline	Activity
	Helpers lined up (timekeeper, microphone runners, scribes)
	Feedback form prepped behind a shortened URL (eg using bit.ly)
	Session registrations closed
	If you are running a hands-on workshop that requires participants having particular software/equipment, send out an email in advance so they can prepare.

Panel discussion checklist

You may have a panel discussion, in which case there are a few extra things to consider:

Timeline	Activity
4 weeks to go	Synopsis done (for website)
	Panellists ready (i.e. briefed and committed)
3 weeks to go	Session Opener's presentation ready and shared
	Questions agreed
1 week to go	Questions printed/written on cards for Moderator
	Slide deck complete
	Helpers lined up (timekeeper, microphone runners, scribes)

Travel and catering

If you have people travelling in from other regions, don't forget their arrangements. Also, don't forget the catering, both daytime and evening! Whatever evening event you have, you will be likely to need to know numbers so that you can book it in.

Make sure enough is done to ensure these parts of the day get as much loving attention as the rest of it.

Timeline	Activity
10 weeks to go	Travellers confirmed and travel planning initiated Trains/flights, hotels, taxis, etc booked
8 weeks to go	Type and location of evening event decided Evening invitations sent out to everyone with RSVP to enable booking (include question about dietary requirements) Email asking everyone (in particular the event participants) for dietary requirements for the daytime catering sent
6 weeks to go	Evening RSVPs closed and venue/catering booked
4 weeks to go	Catering finalised: breakfast, lunch, mid-morning and mid-afternoon snacks and drinks, pre-party drinks

Other

There are always a few extra bits and pieces that someone needs to catch so they don't fall through the gaps. Here are some examples:

Timeline	Activity
4 weeks to go	Music sourced for downtime slots
3 weeks to go	Cameras ready, with sufficient space for photos Loan laptops you might need on the day booked

Post-event

Some suggested follow-up activities to ensure it ends gracefully and lives on fondly in people's memories:

Timeline	Activity
1 week after	Videos edited end uploaded
	Big mention in the department's weekly newsletter
	"Thank you" emails sent to external speakers
	Thanks sent to all volunteers
	Feedback surveys sent out (attendees and participants)
2 weeks after	Internal blog post written
	External blog post written
	Videos and photos uploaded to the conference website
	Bills paid for catering, venue hosting, etc.
3 weeks after	Retrospective held by the organising team to capture lessons for next time:
	Reference feedback from surveys, from real-time retro, and own perspective on what worked/didn't and the lasting impact

Example budget

Here is an example budget for an internal tech conference for 300 attendees:

Category	Item	Unit cost (€)	Total Cost (€)	Notes
Venue	Room hire	300	300	
Venue	Exclusive use	100	100	
Venue	WiFi	600	600	
Food	Lunch	30	9,000	300 attendees
Food	Coffee and tea	3	900	300 attendees
Food	Drinks	10	3,000	300 attendees
Travel	Flights for remote workers	300	6,000	20 remote staff
Travel	Train / Tram	15	4,500	300 attendees
Media	Videography	1,500	1,500	
Media	Photography	400	400	
Media	Printed materials	2	600	300 attendees
Swag	Speaker gift	12	144	12 speakers
Swag	Attendee gift	3	900	300 attendees
	TOTAL		**27,944**	

Remember to include the cost of any interpreters, or live captioning, depending on attendee requirements.

Example promotion plan

As soon as you decide to run an event, you will start to let people know about it in order to attract speakers and to encourage managers to keep calendars free. Once the event starts to draw near though you will want to start generating excitement in the department - you need your attendees to feel the buzz! Plan this out in advance and ensure someone in your organising team has responsibility for driving it.

Here is a suggested schedule of promotional activities:

Timeline	Area	Activity
8 weeks to go	Website	Build and launch your website (see later section for example structure)
-	Scheduling	Send invitations to block out calendars
-	Swag	Decide what swag to provide and who to make it
4 weeks to go	Posters	Confirm info to go on posters (See the next section for examples of what to add)
-	Newsletter	Get a mention in the department newsletter that the conference is 4 weeks away. Include a link to the website
-	Swag	Send designs and order to swag suppliers
3 weeks to go	Posters	Send design brief to your poster designer. Request permission (if needed) to put up printed and digital posters.

Timeline	Area	Activity
-	Social Media	Create Slack (or other team chat tool) channel for people to start asking questions/seeing updates
2 weeks to go	Newsletter	Make sure the next departmental newsletter has a big feature on your conference
-	Social Media	Hype up your conference on department social media/chat channels using info from website
-	Social Media (external)	Build some hype on Twitter if you want to let people know about life at your organisation
1 week to go	Posters	Put up printed posters. Put digital posters on team/department/foyer/any available screens
-	Social Media	Start posting daily reminders on chat channels
-	Swag	Confirm that any swag has been received

Example poster

Like this A3-printable example from the FT, your poster should be big, bold, colourful - and contain *just enough* information to help people:

1. Get to the right place at the right time and
2. Entice people to your website to discover more

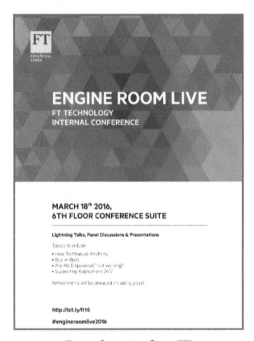

Example poster from FT

Example website sitemap

Here is a suggested structure for an internal website or set of wiki pages:

- Homepage
  - Code of Conduct
- Schedule
  - Programme
  - Speakers
- Remote Access
- Materials
  - Videos
  - Photos
  - Slides
  - Blogs
- Past Events
  - 2018
  - 2017
- Contact
  - Feedback

Homepage

Display basic at-a-glance information, including the event date, location, social media links and tags. Also, post your vision here - why should people come along to the day?

Code of Conduct

The Code of Conduct (see above) is applicable to all attendees, as well as participants. Display this on the website so that people know what is expected of them, and what support is available should they experience anything undesirable.

Schedule

This is the timetable with all speaking and discussion slots, including breaks for refreshments.

- Clearly reflect the multiple streams if you have them
- Clearly indicate the session duration and format
- Link through to the programme and speaker bios
- Provide a link to where the livestream can be found if you are going to make that available.

Programme

Give a short description for each session, with a link to a Speaker bio.

Speakers

Each speaker should have a photograph and a short biography. Link through to their talk in the Programme from here.

Remote access

Explain how to access the conference remotely. How can they interact and how can they report problems?

Materials

Create a placeholder for posting videos (and possibly transcripts), photos, slides and links to blog posts after the event. This will let people know to look out for them afterwards.

Past events

If this is not your first event, preserve and link to the websites for past events (including their artefacts) to act as a reminder to entice people to come along to the next one.

Feedback

Provide the ability to submit feedback on the event. Doing this in advance will mean people can also feedback on some of the preparation/communication activity.

Code of Conduct

Provide a Code of Conduct (CoC) to ensure that the raised energy levels and encouraged debate do not lead to offence. You want some lively interaction but remind people that this is still a professional environment, and they should be mindful of the dangers - and consequences - of not being respectful.

An open-source CoC can be found at confcodeofconduct.com [43], and below is the one used by the FT in their events.

CODE OF CONDUCT

Our conference is a place for free discussion and open exchange of ideas. We can only truly achieve that if everyone involved feels that they are warmly welcomed and valued participants and that they are in a safe environment. Although we may disagree with each other's opinions, we should be able to do so without upsetting or being upset by others.

We therefore do not tolerate verbal comments or presentational material that makes inappropriate use of gender, gender identity and expression, sexual orientation, disability, physical appearance, body size, race, age, or religion. We require participants to respect others' boundaries and do not tolerate deliberate intimidation, stalking, following, harassing photography or recording, disruption of sessions, inappropriate physical contact, or unwelcome sexual attention.

In addition to sharing this in advance with all speakers before they prepare any presentation materials, this should also be displayed on the promotional website and on notices in rooms where sessions will be held.

Because people can be inclined to ignore "small print", it is worth the MC at the start of the day reminding people of the headlines such as "be nice to one another" so that people have this in their minds from the beginning.

How to succeed with tech talks

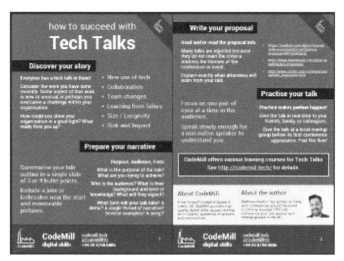

Downloadable guide to succeeding with tech talks - from TechTalksFor-Beginners.net

This guide is adapted from material from Tech Talks for Beginners by Matthew Skelton (techtalksforbeginners.com).

Discover your story

Consider the work you have done recently. Some aspect of that work is new or unusual, or perhaps you overcame a challenge within your organisation. How could you show your organisation in a good light? What really fires you up?

> Consider: New use of tech / Collaboration / Team changes / Learning from failure / Size / Longevity / Risk and Impact

Prepare your narrative: Purpose, Audience, Form

What is the purpose of the talk? What are you trying to achieve? Who is the audience? What is their background and level of knowledge? What will they expect? What form will your talk take? A demo? A single thread of narrative? A series of examples?

> **Summarise your talk outline in a single slide of 3 or 4 bullet points.**

> **Include a joke or icebreaker near the start and memorable pictures.**

Write your talk proposal

First, re-read the proposal information. Many talks are rejected because they do not meet the criteria. Address the themes of the conference or event.

> **Explain exactly what attendees will learn from your talk.**

Practise your talk

Practise the talk in real settings. Give the talk in real-time to your friends, family, or colleagues. Give the talk at a local meetup group before the conference. Feel the flow!

> **Focus on one pair of eyes at a time in the audience.**

> **Speak slowly enough for a non-native speaker to understand you.**

Download a printable PDF of this guidance from techtalksfor-beginners.com

Briefing for panellists

Being on a discussion panel can be a nerve-wracking experience if you've not done it before. In some ways this can seem easier than giving a talk because it doesn't take too much preparation and generally all you have to offer is your opinion. However, having to think on the spot in front of an audience can be daunting. Help them to feel more comfortable by letting them know what to expect.

Here is what was prepared for panelists at the FT's Engine Room event:

BRIEFING FOR PANELLISTS

This briefing is a summary of everything you need to know as a **panellist** or **presenter** at Engine Room 2015.

How the session works

The Moderator will invite the panel to take the stage and introduce them, and there'll be a slide on screen with their smiling faces, names and affiliations, along with a short-link to the selected questions for the session. The Moderator will ask the Session Opener to deliver their introduction.

If you are the Session Opener, you have 5-10 minutes to deliver a **balanced opening talk**, to frame the discussion.

Feel free to talk about your projects, those of the other panellists, the general and specific challenges currently facing the community in that topic area, and suggest some talking points that the audience might want to consider. The talk should assume that the listeners are technically literate but not domain experts in your session subject. If you are writing your talk close enough to the event, use the selected panel questions as a guide to what to cover. [Focus more on **posing questions**, rather than answering them]{.underline}.

When the opening talk is over, the Moderator will ask the first question. The Moderator will have pre-selected around seven 'primary' questions the day before the event. Once the primary question has been asked, the Moderator will take comments from the panel, as well as interventions from the audience, in a relatively freeform way. We limit this to a few minutes, and then move on to our next primary question. Delegates with primary questions will be told their question has been chosen when they arrive. This format is basically a copy of the way the BBC show Question Time works.

Panellists will have always-live mics, so you will be able to jump into the conversation at any time.

The golden rules

Panels can be great ways of bringing people into a conversation, but bad panels can easily be boring, so we'd like all panellists at this event to remember and stick to these rules:

- If you disagree with another panellist, say so. Immediately. If it gets a bit heated, the Moderator is there to calm everyone down, but we'd like to be able to have a frank and open exchange of views rather than polite patience to the point of boredom.

- Keep answers short. **30 seconds is good**. 10 seconds is better. A minute is stretching it. Expect to be cut off by the Moderator if you start blathering.
- Use active debating techniques to make your points more engaging. For example:
  - ask rhetorical questions, or make straw man proposals.
  - Speak in the active voice.
  - Avoid being passive or defensive.
- **Don't dwell on obvious** facts that people can find easily online.
- If in doubt, go as deep and as advanced as possible. **Don't dumb it down**.
- **Don't name-drop without context**. People can easily feel excluded from your circle if they don't know the person you named. Even for well known people, it's easy to say (for example) "Steve Souders, who's probably one of the best known experts in the web performance field, ...".

Recordings and broadcast

We will be recording all the sessions and plan to distribute the video online on our intranet for free after the event.

Timings on the day

We officially start at 9:30am, and tea/coffee will be available from 9:00am. Feel free to come earlier if you'd like.

If you're presenting, please provide your slides as Google slides, PDF, Keynote or HTML slides that we can pre-load onto a shared laptop. Ideally you would email/share these to us in advance :)

Each session is officially an hour long, but we're asking you to finish up about 5 minutes shy of the hour to give us time to change over.

Pre-event briefing

Panellists, moderators, and event organisers will be invited to join us for a briefing prior to the day.

Moderator tips

Moderating a panel needn't be too intimidating a task. However, you do have to keep on top of the discussion and be ready to interrupt people in full flow. Help your Moderator deliver a good panel by giving them some Do's and Don'ts. Here's a selection:

Do...

Do sit amongst your panellists - Have the seats in a slight horseshoe shape. It enables you to make eye contact with all of them, without turning your back on the audience. It's the best position from which to exert control over the proceedings.

Do make sure you're familiar with the questions - Know which panelist you will ask first for each one - and vary it. Have more questions than you think you need in case people don't debate a question as much as you anticipate.

Do be ready to provoke panelists - Whilst you are there to keep the peace if things get heated, the more likely scenario is extreme politeness, so be ready to push the panelists a bit. Here are some tips from Andrew Betts on how to control the conversation: [31]

- Do use leading questions:
    - *"Don't you think it's obvious that asking for permissions up front is a broken experience?"*
- Do use rhetorical questions:
    - *"Are you missing the point?"*
- Do use straw man arguments to amplify points made:
    - *"So Paul, David says you're lying to us."*
- Do use closed questions to draw out specifics:
    - *"Come on, do you support this standard - yes or no?"*
- Do use clarifying questions:
    - *"So you're saying that this is a pointless standard and we should just stop going on about it?"*

Do keep an eye on the time - Be prepared to cut off speakers who have been talking for more than a minute - they have been warned and will accept the interruption. Consider a visible timekeeper in the audience to wave at you after 45 seconds of monologue to help you keep track.

Do seek questions from the audience - Do this throughout, not just at the end. But be clear you're asking for questions only, to encourage them to be brief. And feel free to rephrase them to clarify them for the panel.

Don't...

Don't let the panelists introduce themselves - They'll take too long. If you do it then you can keep it super brief and relevant - 10-20 seconds per panelist is probably long enough.

Don't be scared of asking controversial questions - You've been through the upvoted questions that have been asked, so don't run away from the ones that you think panelists might find hard. They can always promise to "get back to you" if they don't have an answer, but give them the opportunity to rise to the challenge of providing an interesting debate.

Realtime retrospective

The realtime retrospective is a way of capturing feedback or information to enable improvements in real time (as things happen) [51]. The beauty of this is that you don't need much in the way of material or preparation - it's simple!

1. Identify a large wall space, which will be visible to people regularly throughout the day.
2. Mark a horizontal line across the middle, with a rough timeline punctuating it.
3. Provide a stack of sticky notes (proper, sticky ones - don't fall for those cheap ones that don't stick properly or this quickly becomes useless!) and some pens
4. Clearly signpost it with instructions for people to put their thoughts - as they have them - on the wall. Positive above the line, negative below the line.

If you're running agile teams and you've not encountered the realtime retrospective before, consider it for your team-based activities later. It can be a great way of capturing people's thoughts throughout the week before your retrospective session.

> For a good description of the realtime retrospective technique, see Emily Webber's blog post, The Realtime Retrospective [51].

Digital tools to support the organising team

Our case studies have used a wide variety of online tools for collecting Call for Paper submissions, upvoting topics and questions, moderating panels, etc, but here we are faced with the "fast-changing environment" referenced earlier in the book! Many tools used by the organisations no longer exist, or else are likely to vanish at any time.

Those that have been recommended that still exist at time of publishing include:

- Team chat tools to enable comms before and during the event
  - **Slack** was used by the FT, Metaswitch, and Klarna, but there are plenty of others available

- Q&A platform for submitting and upvoting questions (before or during > the event)
  - **Sli.do** was used by the FT to enable audience members to submit and upvote questions to the speaker/panel
  - **Atlassian Confluence** was used by Metaswitch to create some functionality to capture and vote on talk submissions
- Feedback forms
  - **Google Forms** were used by the FT and Klarna to collate talk submissions and event feedback
- Video Conferencing
  - **Zoom** was used by Metaswitch for their video conferencing so that remote teams can connect
  - **Google Hangouts** were used by the FT and Klarna
- Video publishing
  - **YouTube** was used to publish videos of sessions for access by internal employees after the event by the FT and Klarna

Visit the book website for more tools: internaltechconf.com

Online conferences

Since the COVID-19 pandemic of 2019/2020, there has been a big shift to online (remote/virtual) conferences. The key principles for running an internal tech conference are very similar whether the conference is in one physical location or hybrid or all online. However, the technologies and practices for online conferences are evolving at a rapid pace, and it's clear that watching an entire day of live talks from a video call tool is not a good experiene for most people.

We are therefore curating online a set of good practices around online conferences to accompany this book.

> Visit the book website for up-to-date guidance on running online conferences: internaltechconf.com

References

 A full list of references is available on the book website.
Visit InternalTechConf.com for details.

[1] *Internal Tech Conferences - How and Why* (Victoria Morgan-Smith & Matthew Skelton) InfoQ, October 10, 2016. https://www.infoq.com/articles/internal-tech-conferences

[2] *InfoQ. "The InfoQ EMag: Scaling DevOps,"* May 10, 2017. https://www.infoq.com/minibooks/emag-scaling-devops

[3] *Metaswitch blog* https://www.Metaswitch.com/blog

[4] Learning 3.0 http://www.learning30.co/

[5] *How Creative Workers Learn - Developer your career and emergent learning and succeed in the creativity age.* by Alexandre Magno (Happy Melly Express; 1 Oct 2015)) ASIN: B013K8K1CU

[6] Cait O'Riordan https://twitter.com/caitoriordan

[7] *Engine Room Live internal conference 2016* (Victoria Morgan-Smith / FT) http://engineroom.ft.com/2016/05/03/engine-room-live-internal-conference-2016/

[8] Throwable Microphones http://eu.getcatchbox.com/

[9] *Engineering Day Feb 2013 – WebPerf, Service Versioning, Deployments, Chef, and more* (Matthew Skelton / Trainline) https://engineering.thetrainline.com/2012/10/09/engineering-day-lifting-the-bonnet/, https://engineering.thetrainline.com/2013/03/27/engineering-day-feb-2013-webperf-service-versioning-deployments-chef-and-more/

[10] *Internal Tech Conference Toolkit* (Ben Maraney / Klarna) https://engineering.klarna.com/internal-tech-conference-toolkit-79b1ba91bd08

[11] *DOCCON1 – organising a conference* (Rich Haigh / Betfair) https://betsandbits.com/2014/09/23/doccon1-organising-a-conference/

[12] ING at DevOpsDays Amsterdam 2014: *ITIL and DevOps at War in the Enterprise* (Jan Joost-Bouwman) http://www.slideshare.net/JanJoostBouwman/20140620-dev-opsdaysamsterdam-for-publication and *The Journey of devops and continuous delivery in a Large Financial Institution* (Kris Buytaert) http://www.slideshare.net/KrisBuytaert/velocity2013-mh/17?src=clipshare

[13] *Diversity in Tech conferences and Meetups - How and Why* Matthew Skelton (blog), April 28, 2018. https://blog.matthewskelton.net/2018/04/28/diversity-in-tech-conferences-and-meetups-how-and-why/

[14] *Is Gender Diversity Profitable? Evidence from a Global Survey, (Is Gender Diversity Profitable? Evidence from a Global Survey, Feb 2016)* https://piie.com/publications/wp/wp16-3.pdf

[15] PechaKucha https://www.pechakucha.org/faq

[16] *How to help presenters prepare for your conference* (Ben Maraney / Klarna) https://engineering.klarna.com/how-to-help-presenters-prepare-for-your-conference-156d80832caa

[17] *Accessible Conference Guide* (SIG Access) http://www.sigaccess.org/welcome-to-sigaccess/resources/accessible-conference-guide/

[18] *The Annual New Relic Product Offsite Focuses on the Decade Ahead* (Frederic Paul / New Relic) https://blog.newrelic.com/culture/product-offsite-year-of-thinking-big/

[19] *Fearless Change: patterns for introducing new ideas* by Mary Lynn Manns Ph.D & Linda Rising Ph.D (Addison Wesley; 01 edition (4 Oct. 2004)) ISBN 978-0201741575

[20] *Nudge - Improving decisions about health, wealth and happiness* by Richard H. Thaler & Cass R. Sunstein (Penguin Books; 5 Mar 2009) ISBN 978-0141040011

[21] - (removed)

[22] Pearson https://www.pearson.com/uk/

[23] *FT's Engine Room 2015* (Victoria Morgan-Smith / FT) http://engineroom.ft.com/2015/02/25/ft-technology-internal-conference-engine-room-2015/

[24] Nikkei http://www.nikkei.co.jp/nikkeiinfo/en/

[25] Richard Still, FT https://www.linkedin.com/in/richard-still-bb00989/

[26] *Hackathons Motivate Metaswitch and Drive Innovation* (Calum Loudon / Metaswitch) https://www.Metaswitch.com/blog/hackathons-motivate-Metaswitch-and-drive-innovation

[27] *Social capital in the growth of science-and-technology-based SMEs* by Jukka Partanen, Kristian Möller, Mika Westerlund, Risto Rajala, Arto Rajala http://www.sciencedirect.com/science/article/pii/ S0019850108000655

[28] *DOES15 (Re)building an Engineering Culture: DevOps at Target* (Heather Mickman & Ross Clanton / Target) https://www.youtube. com/watch?v=7s-VbB1fG5o

[29] *A Product Manager's visit to the Engine Room* (Mattijas Larsson / FT) http://engineroom.ft.com/2015/03/05/a-product-managers-visit-to-the-engine-room/

[30] *Conferences – jumped up classrooms?* (Donald Clark) http://don-aldclarkplanb.blogspot.co.uk/2008/11/conferences-jumped-up-class-rooms.html

[31] *Better Developer Conferences* (Andrew Betts, August 2017) https:// trib.tv/2017/08/16/better-developer-conferences/

[32] *Review legacy code: Waking dragons is risk worth taking, says Trainline ops head* (Kat Hall) http://www.theregister.co.uk/2016/05/05/ trainline_ops_head_review_code_continuous_lifecycle/

[33] *How TechSmith Rocks Its Internal Developer Conference* (Matthew Heusser / TechSmith) http://www.cio.com/article/2380063/continu-ing-education/how-techsmith-rocks-its-internal-developer-confer-ence.html

[34] *Principles of Sociotechnical Design Revisited* by Albert Cherns, in Human Relations March 1987 vol. 40 no. 3 153-161 http://hum. sagepub.com/content/40/3/153.short

[35] *How to run an internal unconference* (Henrik Kniberg) http:// blog.crisp.se/2013/06/30/henrikkniberg/how-to-run-an-internal-un-conference

[36] *Running Internal Events – The Goat Farm – Episode 5* (Michael Ducy / @mfdii) https://goatcan.do/2015/03/25/running-internal-events-the-goat-farm-episode-5/

[37] *Engineering Day Feb 2013 – WebPerf, Service Versioning, Deployments, Chef, and more* (Trainline Engineering blog, March 2013) https://engineering.thetrainline.com/2013/03/27/engineering-day-feb-2013-webperf-service-versioning-deployments-chef-and-more/

[38] *Reinventing organizations* by Frederic Laloux (Nelson Parker, 2014) ISBN 978-2960133509 https://www.amazon.co.uk/Reinventing-Organizations-Creating-Inspired-Consciousness/dp/2960133501

[39] *The Future of Management Is Teal* (Frederic Laloux) http://www.strategy-business.com/article/00344?gko=10921

[40] *DevOps Handbook* by Gene Kim, Jez Humble, Patrick Debois & John Willis (IT Revolution Press, 2016) ISBN

[41] *Organising the Engine room Conference* (Sarah Wells / FT) http://engineroom.ft.com/2015/03/09/organising-the-engine-room-conference/

[42] *The power of an internal conference - How you can leverage internal experts to build employee engagement* (Thansha Sadacharam) https://medium.com/bridgeable/the-power-of-an-internal-conference-34f9ce6f7dcd

[43] *Conference Code of Conduct* http://confcodeofconduct.com/

[44] How to run a good tech conference by Matthew Skelton https://blog.matthewskelton.net/2018/06/07/how-to-run-a-good-tech-conference/

[45] Skelton, Matthew, and Manuel Pais. Team Topologies. IT Revolution Press, 2019.http://teamtopologies.com/

[46] DORA. "DevOps Research and Assessment." Accessed January 8, 2019.https://devops-research.com/research.html

[47] Rozovsky, Julia. "Re:Work - The Five Keys to a Successful Google Team," November 17, 2015. https://rework.withgoogle.com/blog/five-keys-to-a-successful-google-team/

[48] Forsgren, Nicole, and Jez Humble. *Accelerate: The Science of Lean Software and Devops: Building and Scaling High Performing Technology Organizations.* Portland, Oregon: Trade Select, 2018. pp.101-109

[50] Maraney, Ben. "The Best Developer Conference? Your Own." Klarna Engineering (blog), December 5, 2016. https://engineering. klarna.com/the-best-developer-conference-your-own-ef68f2831b67

[51] Webber, Emily. "The Realtime Retrospective" (blog), November 5, 2016 https://emilywebber.co.uk/the-realtime-retrospective/

[52] British Dyslexia Association, https://www.bdadyslexia.org.uk/ dyslexic/eyes-and-dyslexia

[53] *Why Do We Save the Best for Last?,* by Ben Y Hayden Ph.D., Psychology Today (Oct 24, 2012) https://www.psychologytoday.com/ gb/blog/the-decision-tree/201210/why-do-we-save-the-best-last

[54] Pink, Daniel H. Drive. Main edition. Edinburgh: Canongate Books Ltd, 2011.

[55] Kniberg, Henrik. "Crisp's Blog » What Is an Unconference?" Crisp's Blog (blog), August 30, 2016. https://blog.crisp.se/2016/08/30/ henrikkniberg/what-is-an-unconference

[56] Doing Presentations https://www.doingpresentations.com/

Terminology

- AV - Audio Visual
- Active Voice - specifically referencing an ation eg "John said that", rather than the more passive "it has been said"
- Bootcamp - a short duration working with a software team to gain experience
- CfP - Call for Papers
- Death march - a software project that stretches on at an unsustainable pace and feels destined to fail
- DevOps - an approach to building and running software systems that emphasises close collaboration, flow, long-term team ownership, automation, and metrics
- Diversity and Inclusion - a movement to acknowledge that having a diverse group is insufficient, so inclusion means making it a welcome space for all, not merely a tolerant one
- Echo chamber - a space where a person only encounters views and beliefs similar to their own - likened to a physical echo chamber which is an enclosed space where sound reverberates
- Emergent leadership - leadership being demonstrated by people taking the initiative, rather than be being given a leadership title
- Emergent learning - new knowledge being acquired through experience rather than from formal training courses
- Guild - a cross-team group who meet to share knowledge and experience within a given discipline / competency

- Hack Day - a short, intense period (often a day) for engineers and other disciplines to work together to create a functioning product by the end of the event
- IoT - Internet of Things
- Lightning talk - a short talk of 5 - 10 minutes
- Live captioning - a service that will capture words spoken on a plain text screen as they are said
- NPS - Net Promoter Score
- Open Spaces - self-organised and lightly facilitated discussions
- PechaKucha 20x20 - a lightning talk consisting of 20 slides which autoplay for 20 seconds each
- Psychological Safety - the ability to be oneself with one's team without fear of negative consequence
- Q&A - Questions and Answers
- Rhetorical questions - a figure of speech in the form of a question that is asked to make a point rather than to elicit an answer
- Social capital - a form of currency that is built up through positive social interaction, and which then gets spent in more challenging times. Like any other budget, it needs topped up from time to time.
- Straw Man Proposal - a draft proposal designed to stimulate debate - may be deliberately provocative
- Team stand-ups - a short, usually daily, team meeting to set the focus for the day

Index

CPSIA information can be obtained
at www.ICGtesting.com
Printed in the USA
BVHW091222191120
593717BV00004B/104